# THE PENTATEUCH

# THE PENTATEUCH

*A Study in Salvation History*

ALEXA SUELZER S.P.

HERDER AND HERDER

1964
HERDER AND HERDER NEW YORK
232 Madison Avenue, New York 16, N.Y.

Library of Congress Catalog Card Number: 64-19739
© 1964 by Herder and Herder, Incorporated
Printed in the United States of America

# Contents

# Foreword

IT is safe to say, I think, that no block of sacred literature has had an influence comparable to that of the Pentateuch, the five books of Moses which occupy pride of place in the Jewish canon of sacred Scripture. Both Jews and Christians profess belief in the inspiration of these books, howsoever differently they may explain what they mean by the charism of inspiration. Besides, the Torah provides the basis for Judaism's way of life while any student of Christian theology, Catholic or Protestant, recognizes how deeply the Law and the events surrounding its revelation have entered into the fabric of Christian life and thought.

Given the importance of this body of literature it should surprise no one that, ever since the rise of biblical criticism, most Old Testament scholars have directed their research to one or another aspect of the Pentateuch. To read a survey of Pentateuchal criticism for the past two centuries is to recall the great names in the Old Testament field. It also shows most of these men locked in vigorous debate over basic issues such as the origin, authorship and structure of this fundamental material. If it is possible today to speak cautiously of some "assured results," they are the upshot of a long period of analysis and reflection devoted to Israel's early historical traditions.

The contribution of Catholics to this effort has been a modest one. There is the usual nod in our direction with the remark that the founder of modern Pentateuchal criticism was the

French Catholic physician, Jean Astruc; now it appears certain that he had one or two forerunners whose work had long been forgotten. Whatever may be said about Catholic participation in the beginnings of this movement the fact remains that only with the published studies of that intrepid pioneer, Father Marie-Joseph Lagrange O.P., could we speak of anything like a Catholic response to a biblical criticism which had produced many positive results but which, unfortunately, was often dominated by a bias against the whole supernatural order. It was the merit of Lagrange to see more clearly than others that burying one's head in the sand is not a sound tactic before an enemy which threatens to sweep the field.

Sister Alexa is the latest to enter the lists of Pentateuchal criticism, not to add another chapter to the story of literary analysis (though she has not neglected this), but to give us a sound, critical study of the Pentateuch as a part of God's self-disclosure. The metaphor of "entering the lists" is not altogether appropriate since this is not a work of apologetics but the communication of positive results acquired in research. She has made it clear that, in the Pentateuch, we are not dealing merely with history, but salvation history; she sees in this recounted dialogue between Yahweh and his people the revelation of the gracious purposes he has for all mankind. Chairman of the department of theology at St. Mary-of-the-Woods College, Indiana, and a graduate of the Catholic University, Sister Alexa has brought to her task several years of rigorous training in biblical criticism at the graduate level. The results are here to be read.

In my opinion this is not a book to initiate the beginner into Old Testament studies; on the other hand, it is not intended solely for that distinguished fraternity known as the "professionals." The intelligent professional reader with some previous knowledge of critical method as applied to the Bible will find the book helpful even though it makes demands beyond those of the conventional books of introduction. If this calls for an extra effort it is worth the trouble for Sister Alexa has much to offer toward a better understanding of the Pentateuch. Happily, she never hesitates to admit candidly that there are still problems for which we have no answer. The scholarship, in short, is informed and honest. May this book encourage either Sister Alexa or others to examine along similar lines other parts of the Old Testament.

FREDERICK L. MORIARTY S.J.

*Weston College*

# Abbreviations

| | |
|---|---|
| AAS | *Acta Apostolicae Sedis* |
| AASO | *Annual of the American Schools of Oriental Research* |
| AER | *The American Ecclesiastical Review* |
| ANET | *Ancient Near Eastern Texts Relating to the Old Testament*, ed James B. Pritchard |
| ASS | *Acta Sanctae Sedis* |
| BA | *The Biblical Archaeologist* |
| BASOR | *Bulletin of the American Schools of Oriental Research* |
| Bib | *Biblica* |
| BJRylL | *Bulletin of the John Rylands Library* |
| BZAW | *Beihefte zur Wissenschaft für die alttestamentliche Wissenschaft* |
| CBQ | *The Catholic Biblical Quarterly* |
| CSEL | *Corpus scriptorum ecclesiasticorum latinorum* |
| DAFC | *Dictionnaire apologetique de la foi catholique* |
| DowR | *The Downside Review* |
| ETL | *Ephemerides Theologicae Lovanienses* |
| ExpT | *The Expository Times* |
| HAT | *Handkommentar zum Alten Testament* (Göttingen) |
| HSAT | *Die Heilige Schrift des Alten Testaments* (Bonn) |
| HUCA | *Hebrew Union College Annual* |
| Interpr | *Interpretation* |

| | |
|---|---|
| IsrEJ | *The Israel Exploration Journal* |
| JBL | *The Journal of Biblical Literature* |
| JBR | *The Journal of Bible and Religion* |
| JNES | *The Journal of Near Eastern Studies* |
| JR | *The Journal of Religion* |
| JSemS | *The Journal of Semitic Studies* |
| LXX | Septuagint |
| MT | Masoretic text |
| NRT | *Nouvelle revue théologique* |
| PL | *Patrologia latina, Migne* |
| RB | *Revue biblique* |
| RGG³ | *Die Religion in Geschichte und Gegenwart*, 3d ed |
| RScPhTh | *Revue des sciences philosophiques et théologiques* |
| RSS | *Rome and the Study of Scripture*, ed Conrad Louis |
| S | Samaritan Pentateuch |
| Scr | *Scripture* |
| SZ | *Stimmen der Zeit* |
| TS | *Theological Studies* |
| VD | *Verbum Domini* |
| VDBS | *Dictionnaire de la Bible: Supplément* (Vigouroux) |
| VT | *Vetus Testamentum* |
| VTS | *Vetus Testamentum: Supplementum* |
| ZAW | *Zeitschrift für die alttestamentliche Wissenschaft* |

# Introduction

Why should the Christian, the Catholic, read the Bible? More specifically why read the Pentateuch? The question is legitimate. For Catholics the Bible is not an absolute—neither the Old nor the New Testament, nor both together. It has a divine authority and a permanent message but it is not the rule of faith. Although Christians of early centuries did not make the modern distinction between Scripture and tradition they were aware nonetheless that the Old Testament (to which the present work is limited) is not necessary for faith or salvation. Why should they read the Scripture of the old dispensation? Their reply was determined by the age in which they lived: the Old Testament is primarily a preparation for the New; the Old Testament finds its fulfillment in the New. In order to maintain the uniqueness of the Christian economy without rejecting the Old Testament exegetes searched the Scripture for spiritual meanings. In applying Augustine's dictum: "Not only is the New Testament enfolded in the Old, but the Old is unfolded in the New" (CSEL 28, 2, 141), they made typological interpretation their paramount concern. Such exegesis is both valid and valuable; as used by the Fathers it penetrates the innermost meaning of the divine word. The modern exegete also sees the Old Testament as type and Christ as antitype. But recent advances in all fields of biblical study have opened vistas undreamed by earlier scholars and have effected a renewed interest in the

13

literal sense of the Bible. As a result the modern student of Scripture seeks to confront the text and wrest the meaning, however limited and imperfect, that the words had for the sacred author.

Polemic needs of a later day (a day not yet ended) made of the Old Testament a rich quarry for the hewing of citations to fill dogmatic or apologetic needs. The use of Scripture in the formulation of theological theses can limit or distort a text if there is no regard for its context. Sometimes the desire to verify a doctrinal formulation blunts the fact that the divine disclosure was a gradual historical process and not a ready-made set of divine pronouncements that were handed down at one particular moment in history. Utilizing the Old Testament solely as a repertory of proofs does not contribute to an understanding of the word of God. Therefore the Christian approach to the Bible should be determined not by the needs of apologetics or dialectics but by the desire to enter into the vital, personal relationship God has established between man and himself, a record of which he has given us in the Bible.

The Old Testament is of course incomplete and fragmented. But the completion of the Old Testament by the New is not merely a matter of matching type with antitype or text with text. The New Testament fulfills the Old in that it is the perfect unfolding of a divine revelation which was previously inchoate, halting and gradual. For practical ends Christianity can dispense with the Old Testament, but tradition that is truly Christian cannot fully understand itself if unaware of its bonds with the ancient traditions of the Hebrews. The affinity of the testaments is not limited to an historical relationship; rather the connection is so vital that the one can be fully comprehended only in the light of the other. The living reality of the gospels is inextricably bound up with the Old Testament as with a past which was already pointing to future fulfillment. A knowledge of the

14

ways of God in times past makes possible a keener response to the salvation he now accomplishes through his Son.

The heart of the Bible then lies in its record of God's activity in history. The Pentateuch perhaps more than any other portion of the Old Testament reveals Yahweh as the God who acts; for what else is salvation history but the story of Yahweh's deeds, the deeds which bring salvation to all men? The Hebrews only gradually came to understand Yahweh's relations with his people, and his intervention in their affairs was epitomized in the traditions of the Exodus and Sinai. Can the reader therefore extract the essence of salvation history from those chapters in the Book of Exodus dealing with these divine interventions par excellence? If so then a study of the entire Pentateuch would be unnecessary. But the Hebrews were not content with a stark recital of the events central to Yahwism. What happened in the Exodus and at Sinai never hardened into static memories; rather each generation reworked and reinterpreted its heritage of traditions, understood itself anew as Israel faced with the privileges and responsibilities of divine election. Thus the Deuteronomist, writing hundreds of years after the events at Sinai, was not merely indulging a penchant for historical atmosphere when he cried: "Hear, O Israel, the statutes and decrees which I proclaim in your hearing *this day*" (Dt 5:1); or "I set before you here, *this day*, a blessing and a curse" (Dt 11:26). Yahweh's activity admits no temporal limits and his continuing offer of the covenant demands a fresh response from each generation.

So considered, salvation history cannot be compassed by a summary core of historical "facts." Only in modern times has the true nature of the Pentateuch as a synthesis of long-evolving traditions been recognized. For centuries biblical exegetes regarded the Books of Moses as an historical account of Yahweh's dealings with mankind from the creation until the tribal settlement in Palestine. So long as this view was retained the full import of Yahweh's impingement on history could not be realized. In other words salvation history can be understood only if the Pentateuch is viewed as the end result of Israel's gradual realization of the meaning of Yahweh's revelation and presence in history. Modern biblical criticism has made such an approach possible. It is to the credit of nineteenth and twentieth century scholars that they have denoted the multifold strands of tradition intertwined in the Pentateuch. And although they have sometimes gone to excess in their interpretations of the Books of Moses these scholars have nonetheless succeeded in showing how the Pentateuch came to be, and in the process they have broadened and deepened the concept of salvation history.

The nineteenth century documentary theory—classic Wellhausenism—was the culmination of two centuries of exploration and analysis of the Pentateuchal materials. By 1885 the literary methods of higher criticism had arrived at four principal documents universally acknowledged in liberal Protestant circles: the Yahwist, the Elohist, the Deuteronomic and the Priestly. The Yahwist document, most ancient of the components, was considered no older than the ninth century; the youngest, the Priestly writing, was regarded as the product of the postexilic Jewish community. A natural consequence of the discovery of these individual documents of late origin was of course the denial of Mosaic authorship, for, though there were some isolated ancient traditions within the writings, no one of the documents could possibly date back to Moses.

This denial of Mosaic authorship rendered the documentary theory anathema to orthodox Protestants and to Catholics. In addition the association of the theory with the chief features of nineteenth century scholarship—rationalism and its rejection of the supernatural, historicism and Hegelian philosophy—led to its rejection by Catholics. Decrees of the Pontifical Biblical Commission in 1906 strongly asserted Moses' role in the composition of the Pentateuch, but subsequent comments on the decrees, as in the Biblical Commission's reply to Cardinal Suhard in 1948, have considerably broadened (without defining) the concept of the substantial authorship attributed to Moses. Protestant scholarship on the other hand has returned to a more moderate position, with many critics now acknowledging the possibility that portions of the Pentateuch may date back to Mosaic times and may even have Moses for their author.

The documentary theory was not content merely to shake the foundations of Yahwism by challenging its Mosaic origin. The late dating of the individual documents and the assignation of the definitive Pentateuch to postexilic times changed the entire complexion of biblical studies by placing the prophets before the Pentateuch and by making them the originators of ethical monotheism.

The initial success of the documentary hypothesis created a false hope that the secret of Pentateuchal origins would be disclosed as soon as critics had efficiently performed the task of sorting the Books of Moses into their components. Soon however it became obvious that the separation of the documents was only a first step. Does the assignment of pericopes to documentary sources bring the critic any nearer the explanation of their origin and subsequent amalgamation? What lies beyond J, E, D and P? Form criticism under the guiding genius of Hermann Gunkel sought answers to these questions. Gunkel acknowledged that literary critics are quite correct in their analyses of the chief documents in the Pentateuch; each writing however is only the starting point for much deeper research; the documents are the climax, the definitive stage of traditions which circulated orally for great lengths of time, constantly being pruned, expanded, transformed. The document as such is not the critic's concern; what matters is the vital moment—the life setting—giving birth to traditions which have come to their

17

full flower in the written document. The search for this life setting became one of the principal concerns of form criticism, for concrete situations in the life of the community determined the genesis of particular traditions and guided their later development.

The better understanding of the role of oral tradition in the preservation and growth of the Pentateuchal materials has simultaneously effected an appreciation of the fluid, dynamic character of Israel's reflections upon her encounter with Yahweh. In its drive toward universal concepts modern criticism has often sought to crystallize Israel's belief, to arrest it within a moment of time by a tidy series of principles and propositions. But the attempt to systematize salvation history is always a betrayal of Israel's relation to Yahweh, for Hebrew religion is essentially dynamic. A new generation received the traditions of its fathers not as a rigid account of a meeting with Yahweh accomplished once and for all at a particular historical moment, but as a heritage which it had to vitalize and develop by personal response. The central core of traditions always retained the same fundamental note; in the course of time the overtones of this fundamental note became more resonant and more varied as successive generations rethought and reapplied past experiences. With the continual expansion of the primary indubitable encounters with Yahweh the deposit of sacred tradition grew steadily richer and more complex, with emphasis now on one, now on another facet of Yahweh's action and his people's response. As combined in the Pentateuch the traditions emanating from different sources for more than a millennium portray Israel's elaborated thinking on salvation history: a realization of God acting in history, God coming to men he created and asking of them a response which is at the same time their salvation.

The methods of literary and form criticism can trace the

18

growth of Israel's traditions with some degree of accuracy. Such analytic investigations however cannot explain the final synthesis of the materials in the Pentateuch as we know it. The complete and finished picture of Old Testament faith was not granted all at once but was fashioned piece by piece into the mosaic of full Old Testament revelation. In the composition of the Pentateuchal portions of that picture the sacred writers used the most varied literary materials—popular tales, songs, legends, genealogies, legal corpora; yet the Pentateuch is no haphazard amalgamation. It is rather a collection of traditions carefully selected and edited for the presentation of salvation history, i.e. history directed by Yahweh for the realization of Israel's destiny. The organic unity of the Pentateuch derives from this rockbed conviction of Yahweh's choice of Israel as his own people, and faith in this conviction was a primary factor in the growth of the Pentateuchal materials. The principles guiding the writers in their choice and treatment of traditions cannot with any certainty be established; nevertheless it is clear that faith was at work, giving to the most disparate traditions a characteristic stamp and orientation. The materials were in flux until the time of their final redaction, continually receiving fresh nuances —but always under the influence of faith. This firm control of the traditions during the long stages of their development suggests a cultic life setting for their origin and growth. Recurring festal celebrations were occasions for the reactualization of salvation history. As the tribes gathered to honor Yahweh at the cultic centers they listened to recitations of the historical deeds through which Yahweh revealed himself and his will to Israel. They then experienced for themselves this history as it was made available to them in cultic actions, and bound themselves again to Yahweh by renewal of the convenant.

From earliest times in Israel the events of the Exodus and Sinai, traditions vital to Israel's faith, stood out as the hard core of this history and were normative even in the preliterary stages of the Pentateuch. These basic themes were expanded and enriched by subordinate motifs, e.g. the traditions of oppression in Egypt that were attached to the Exodus or the stories of the desert wandering that join the Exodus accounts with the Sinai revelation. As an introduction to the conquest of the land promised in the Exodus and to the covenant inaugurated on Sinai the theme of the patriarchal promises traces the election of Israel back to Yahweh's choice of Abraham and his posterity. The primitive history, a theological interpretation of the world in relation to God, serves as a kind of prelude to the redemptive activity of Yahweh unfolded in the patriarchal history, in the deliverance from bondage and in the alliance at Sinai.

Intertwined with these narrative themes of salvation history is extensive legislation, imbedded for the most part in the Sinai revelation. Although subordinate to the main themes and certainly less interesting, this legislation cannot be passed over if there is to be an adequate survey of the Pentateuch. By its sheer bulk alone the law demands attention: almost half the Pentateuchal books concern law. Moreover the vast legal stretches of the Pentateuch are perhaps its most striking if not its most formidable aspect. Much of this law can be dispensed with, though not of course before the omissions have been justified. Other portions of legislation require greater consideration because of their intimate relation to the convenant or their perdurance in Christian morality. A second reason commends the study of biblical law: the stress in late Judaism on law as an absolute and the characterization of the Old Testament as a dispensation dominated by legalism have obscured and distorted the pristine tenor of Hebrew law. An analysis of the origin, scope and force of biblical law will balance undue emphasis upon law and temper exaggerated judgments about its position in Yahwism.

20

Finally the narrative themes and the legal corpora are the primary vehicles of God's saving plan and as such they can be utilized to draw from the Pentateuch its message of salvation. And the objection that the isolation of the major motifs places an artificial schematism on the Pentateuch is far from valid. In stressing the principal themes we are but following the example of the sacred writers themselves, who synthesized the manifold traditions at their disposal. Thus did they retain, despite the gigantic proportions of the definitive Pentateuch, a primary accent on the central message of the Pentateuchal revelation: Yahweh has entered history to bring salvation to men.

1

# Themes of the Pentateuchal Narratives

## Introduction

THE partition of the Pentateuch into the individual books of Moses was a practical measure undertaken to render the massive work more manageable and intelligible. The essential unity of the work as a whole however was not impaired, for no matter what additions and redactions the Pentateuch underwent it ever retained a basic constant in the light of which disparate traditions were eliminated, adapted or transformed. That normative was the Hebrews' vital experience of Yahweh effecting his will for all men and for Israel in particular; hence the traditions chosen by the sacred writers for preservation in the Pentateuch are all aspects of the dominant thesis: Yahweh's salvific deeds and Israel's response. Some scattered traditions reflect isolated elements of the theme; others, like facets having similar angles of reflection, converge their light on a particular phase, reinforcing and clarifying a single aspect of the leitmotif. No single treatment can hope to display all the facets of the Pentateuch; therefore in our selection of materials we will follow the sacred writers and stress the themes they hold paramount in Israel's account of her salvation history.

What are the salient motifs in the salvation history? The

Pentateuchal materials are grouped around major traditions which include theologized reflections about Yahweh in his relation to Israel: Yahweh, creator of the world, effected his plan for man's salvation by calling apart the patriarchs and promising them land and posterity. Later he rescued the children of the patriarchs from Egyptian slavery, guided them through hardships in the desert, climaxed his deeds by a personal alliance at Sinai and at last brought his people to the land he had pledged to their fathers. The motifs here so tersely recapitulated developed from slender beginnings; in the process of growth they absorbed and reshaped the most diverse materials until the basic themes blossomed into a work of gigantic theological proportions. The exact process of this growth is one of the key problems in Pentateuchal studies.

Strictly speaking the primitive history (Gn 1–11) is an introduction to the salvation history, not one of its themes. In this study however it is treated with the other motifs because it provides a background—the theological realities and the Semitic world—against which the salvation drama unfolds with added depth and clarity. The drama begins with the choice of Abraham and the promise of land[1] and progeny to him and his descendants. The stories of the fathers bring out the sovereignty of the divine will; with equal freedom Yahweh employs or rejects human instruments and for the most part accomplishes his designs by what seem to be the ordinary ways of Providence. But in the Exodus Yahweh's action is of a different sort altogether; here he is a God of obvious power: "Or did any god venture to go and take a nation for himself from the midst of another nation, by testings, by signs and wonders, by war, with his strong hand and outstretched arm, and by great terrors, all of which the Lord, your God, did for you in Egypt before your very eyes?" (Dt 4:34). The vivid memory of delivery from bondage

23

was the germinal cell from which grew Israel's fuller realization of Yahweh as pre-eminently her God.

In return for the divine goodness which had wrought her deliverance from Egypt Israel showed surly ingratitude. The stories of the desert wandering with their alternate themes of divine solicitude and human caviling sharpen the contrast between the largesse of Yahweh and the niggardly response of Israel to her God. Yet at Sinai—his will to save unchanged by his children's ingratitude—Yahweh concluded a covenant with Israel, thus binding himself irrevocably to his people. The covenant will be treated more fully in the discussion of Hebrew law; for the present it will suffice to place the Sinai revelation in its proper context and to relate it to the other themes of salvation history.

The traditions included in the themes are far more than cherished memories of the past. They bear the revelation of the Lord and, although rooted in the temporal order, they have validity for all generations and present to Israel of every age a renewed challenge of total response to the divine election. The sacred writers generally develop a given theme within defined limits of a book, e.g. the promises to the patriarchs in Gn 12–50. Within a particular theme however numerous isolated traditions may occur, e.g. Gn 14; these have been omitted or referred to only in passing in order to strengthen the impact of the theme in question. Where a key motif treated in one section is enhanced by echoes elsewhere in the Pentateuch (e.g. Dt's frequent mention of the promises made to the patriarchs), these references have been incorporated into the treatment of the main theme.

## The primitive history

The primitive history of Gn 1–11 stands at the head of the Pentateuch as a background for the greatly expanded traditions of the patriarchs, the Exodus and Sinai, in which are recapitulated Yahweh's merciful designs. As the traditions of salvation history burgeoned, the sacred writers felt the need to trace the antecedents of Israel's election by describing Yahweh's relation to the world from its creation until the time of Abraham. Living as she did in an atmosphere permeated by myths about cosmic and human origins Israel at an early age must have formed her own cosmogony relating the creation of the world to Yahweh. However, creation accounts in written form appear only late in Israel's history. Apparently long theological reflection was required to correlate the traditions of origins with her prime interest: the portrayal of Yahweh's action in history. Properly speaking there is no Hebrew doctrine of creation, for nowhere is creation treated for itself; the creation account is only an introduction to the saving plan initiated by the call of Abraham. Creation was seen as an historical event opening the course of human existence, a fact stressed in the careful chronology of the Priestly writer.

It may seem that Gn 1–11 has already received its due meed of attention in dogmatic and apologetic writings. The chapters of the primitive history have played a vital part in the development and exposition of such doctrines as creation, grace, original justice, concupiscence and original sin. Catholic apologetes, furthermore, must consider the relation of the biblical recital of human origins to modern scientific theories. The day has passed when apologetes can be flustered by supposed conflicts between the Bible and biological evolution; but there is still a legitimate need to examine contemporary hypotheses of cosmic and human origins in the light of Church teaching, which is based in part on the biblical accounts. Our present concern however is not with such a use of biblical materials. It frequently happens that when the Bible is used for doctrinal, moral or apologetic content inherent in a later stage of revelation the

25

sacred accounts are not permitted to yield their true and complete message; they are not considered in and for themselves but only in relation to some other interest or concern. Our study, untrammeled by direct dogmatic or apologetic preoccupations, will let the narratives relate for themselves the significance the events described in Gn 1–11 held for the sacred writer—and hence for Israel as a whole.

## Creation

The different cycles of tradition present in the Pentateuch are immediately obvious in the double creation accounts: the Priestly narrative of Gn 1:1–2,4a and the Yahwist version of 2:4b–25. The Priestly writer conceives creation as development from chaos to cosmos; he emphasizes the intial *tōhû wābōhû,* the formlessness and utter lack of distinction; and in an orderly framework of seven days he describes the constitution and adornment of the world in which man appears as the climax. The first words of Gn seem to be a summary of the story to follow: the visible world owes its origin to God. Although creation out of nothing is not explicit in the Priestly narrative it might be implied. It is also true that the verb *bara'* is reserved for the divine activity, and no reference to the material used ever accompanies it. For the Yahwist, creation is progress from the desert to the sown: "There was not yet any field shrub on the earth nor had the plants of the field sprung up, for the Lord God had sent no rain on the earth and there was no man to till the soil" (2:5). From the very beginning of the Yahwist report man is the center of attention and the process of creation is complete only when "the Lord God took the man and placed him in the garden of Eden to till it and to keep it" (2:15).

Both writers emphasize that the world and all it contains are the work of Yahweh; but the Priestly writer stresses Yahweh's effortless and transcendent creation by a mere word ("God said, 'Let there be light,' and there was light" [Gn 1:3]). Even where the Priestly writer uses the phrase "God made," as in Gn 1:16, it is preceded by the divine creative word, as if to say that all things were effected by the power of his word. The Yahwist on the contrary conceives Yahweh as a potter fashioning man from clay and then breathing into his nostrils the breath of life (2:7). The sole reference to the creation of woman in the Priestly narrative is the brief text: "Male and female he created them" (1:27). The Yahwist however regards the creation of woman as the definite climax of his story in ch 2. He views woman as the equal of man because she is of the same nature and is given by Yahweh to be man's helpmate, not his chattel. If the report in Gn 2:7 of the creation of Adam is not a literal description of how the first man came to be, it would also seem that the account of the creation of Eve is not to be taken literally, but rather as an analogy illustrating the writer's thoughts on the nature of woman and her relation to man.

Gn 1–2 contains some elements common to ancient pagan mythologies and these common elements raise the question: what is the relationship between creation myths of the ancient Near East and the story of creation in Gn? Critics of an earlier time dismissed the biblical narratives as Hebrew modifications of older creation myths; nowadays the question cannot be answered so simply. Since certain parallels to Gn are found in *Enuma elish,* a dramatic recital of the struggle between cosmic order and chaos, a brief summary of the Akkadian epic will reveal points of resemblance and contrast. In the strife among the gods (begotten by the primordial Apsu and Tiamat, fresh and salt waters respectively) Marduk cuts in two the defeated Tiamat and uses her body to form the heavens and the earth. Then the victorious Marduk discloses his plan:

27

Blood I will mass and cause bones to be.
I will establish a savage, "man" shall be his name.
Verily, savage-man I will create.
He will be charged with the service of the gods
That they might be at ease (6:5–8).

The god Kingu who had incited Tiamat to rebellion is selected:

They bound him, holding him before Ea.
They imposed on him his guilt and severed his blood (vessels).
Out of his blood they fashioned mankind.
He imposed the service and let free the gods (6:31–34).

The *Enuma elish* obviously has rough parallels with the Gn creation account; doubtless Tiamat is related etymologically to the abyss (*tᵉhôm*) of Gn 1:2 and the formation of man from the blood of a god recognizes godlike characteristics in man, characteristics which Gn attributes to his being made in the image and likeness of God. The tenor of the biblical narrative is so distinctive however and the method and purpose of the creation it describes so different that a real dependence of Gn on Babylonian mythology is inconceivable. The gross polytheism of the *Enuma elish* and its atmosphere of struggle between hostile forces are totally absent from Gn, where Yahweh as sole creator accomplishes his works effortlessly by omnipotent decrees.[2] No suggestion of creation from nothing is found in the pagan myths because the "creation" is always achieved with pre-existent materials—the body of Tiamat or the blood of Kingu. In contrast to the idea that man was created for the service of the gods both the Yahwist and Priestly traditions portray Adam as the object of Yahweh's personal concern. He is surrounded with every good, blessed and made fruitful; by his dominion over the earth he is even permitted to share the divine creativity.

It is clear then that the resemblance of Gn 1–2 to older creation myths is limited chiefly to conceptualization. Although the sacred writer was inspired he did not necessarily receive his materials by revelation. In fact revelation, either primitive or direct, should be excluded as the source of the creation story. (This exclusion does not however extend to the role of revelation in the formation of the story.) As he fashioned his story of the primeval world the author may have employed literary forms well known to his audience, just as a modern author writes in the familiar genre of the novel or play to convey his thought. In using ancient literary forms the biblical writer deliberately freed them from their mythological dimensions and concepts. Thus the Priestly writer's casual description of the sun and moon as two great lights and his stress upon their limited function (Gn 1:14–19) are possibly a polemic directed against the worship of these luminaries as depicted in the mythic materials. The Priestly description is more subtle but perhaps no less effective than Dt's direct prohibition: "And when you look up to the heavens and behold the sun or moon or any star among the heavenly hosts, do not be led astray into adoring them or serving them" (Dt 4:19). Again, the organization of old materials into a seven-day framework lifts the story from the realm of myth into the temporal order and presents creation as a definite historic act.

This appeal to resemblances in literary form is not intended to oversimplify the relation between Gn and myth, for, as the Biblical Commission noted in its reply to Cardinal Suhard, the question of genres in the primeval history is obscure and complex; "one can, therefore, neither deny nor affirm their historicity without unduly attributing to them the canons of a literary style within which it is impossible to classify them."[3] It is evident however that the creation accounts are not meant as a literal description of events as they actually transpired but as analogies which the sacred writer used to express the burden of his thought: Yahweh alone created all that exists, arranged it in a suitable order and climaxed his work by the creation of man and woman in his own image.

29

## Temptation and fall

One theological concern of the Priestly writer is to demonstrate that all of Yahweh's creation is good; seven times he repeats the refrain "God saw that it was good." Given the transcendent perfection of Yahweh the creator it is unthinkable that his works can be anything but perfect. Nevertheless the world has degenerated from its pristine goodness. Having described cosmic and human origins in his introduction to salvation history the sacred author must now explain how deterioration in man and in the world came about. Why must man painfully wrest a living from the earth he was meant to dominate; why does a woman bear her children in travail and sorrow; why do death and decay await man at the end? Where does sin come from? In answering these questions the Yahwist rejects the notion that a primal principle of evil exists in the world. Evil is an intrusion; originally it had no place in the goodness of Yahweh's creation. Here too the story of how sin, suffering and death entered the world need not be a literal report of what actually happened. Sin and its consequences are the burden of the message; the vehicle of the message could well be familiar genres appealing to the imagination as well as to the mind.

The Yahwist conceives all suffering and death as the result of man's disobedience to Yahweh's decree not to eat the fruit of the tree of knowledge of good and evil (Gn 2:17). Gn 2:9 also speaks of the tree of life, which is not mentioned again until 3:22. The two trees perhaps represent a double tradition in the Yahwist narrative. (The dirge over the king of Tyre in Ez 28:11–19 is based on still another tradition of the paradise story, one in which there is no mention of woman.) The temptation and fall are recorded with great psychological insight. The serpent offers a casual opening gambit: "Did God say, 'You shall not eat of any tree of the garden?'" (3:1). The woman exaggerates the divine prohibition; the serpent pursues the issue until "the woman saw that the tree was good for food, pleasing to the eyes, and desirable for the knowledge it would give. She took of its fruit and ate it, and also gave some to her husband and he ate" (3:6–7).

Although an exact determination of their sin is impossible the context of the story gives some clues to its nature. The serpent assures Eve that eating from the forbidden tree will bring knowledge, not death: "You will be like God, knowing good and evil" (Gn 3:5). Then after the fall Yahweh says: "Indeed! the man has become like one of us, knowing good and evil" (3:22). What does it mean, to know good and evil? The Hebrew idiom used in 3:5 and 3:22 can be interpreted as totality of knowledge. The context suggests another meaning: by disobedience Adam and Eve tried to attain familiarity with mysteries beyond their human status; they set themselves as arbiters of the moral order, thus usurping Yahweh's prerogatives. Thomas Aquinas notes that man sinned by coveting the likeness of God as regards good and evil, so that with his own native powers he might decide good and evil for himself (S th, II, II, 163, a. 1). Neither of these interpretations however sheds light on the nature of the transgression.

A third connotation identifies knowledge of good and evil with some kind of sexual experience. Certainly normal intercourse between the sexes cannot be meant, although some scholars have so interpreted the texts.[4] The tenor of the narrative of the creation of Adam and Eve indicates that the union of the sexes is planned and blessed by Yahweh (see Gn 1:27ff; 2:21ff). Nevertheless, in the face of the excesses of Canaanite fertility cults with their exaltation of the female principle, the sacred writer could have conceived the primal sin as a perversion of lawful sexual activity. The relation between vv 5 and 7 in ch 3 strengthens the possibility of this interpretation. The ser-

31

pent's promise: "Your eyes will be opened, and you will be like God" is echoed and expanded in v 7: "Then the eyes of both were opened, and they realized that they were naked" (see also 3:11). At first glance an interpretation of the sin as a sexual offense may seem improbable because the knowledge acquired is supposed to make Adam and Eve like God, who in Hebrew thought is never associated with sexual activity. The difficulty disappears with the realization that fertility cults had as one of their objectives communion with divinity. Further the serpent was used as a sexual symbol in the ancient Near East, and it is possible that the author of the biblical narratives was so employing it. The identity of the serpent is never fully clarified; he represents man's enemy, also Yahweh's foe, but he remains a creature nonetheless.

The aftermath of the transgression is portrayed with equal psychological accuracy. Adam gives Yahweh the faltering explanation: "The woman you placed at my side gave me fruit from the tree and I ate" (Gn 3:12); then Eve in turn excuses herself: "The serpent deceived me and I ate" (3:13). Punishment is inevitable; yet before he decrees it Yahweh addresses a curse to the serpent:

Because you have done this, cursed are you among all animals, and among all the beasts of the field; on your belly you shall crawl, dust shall you eat, all the days of your life. I will put enmity between you and the woman, between your seed and her seed; he shall crush your head, and you shall lie in wait for his heel (3:14–15).

The phrase "you and the woman" applies literally to the serpent and Eve; "her seed" is the descendants of Adam and Eve. The seed of the serpent is less easily determined; it is probably a literary expression of resistance to God by all created forces of evil. The picture in v 15b ("He shall crush [šûf] your head and you shall lie in wait for [šûf] his heel") is one of perpetual struggle between the seed of Eve and that of the serpent. Within the context of the Yahwist's sin-deliverance theme however the words indicate more than a continuing, indecisive conflict and one can assume ultimate victory for mankind. In addition Gn 3:14–15 is from first to last a curse addressed to the serpent; this fact also permits an interpretation of final defeat for the tempter of mankind.[5]

The punishments meted out by Yahweh touch Adam and Eve in the activities most proper to them. Man's easy dominion over the earth is now at an end; henceforth he will eat its fruit only in sweat and toil. As for woman not only will pain and distress accompany her childbearing, but her longing for man will serve to increase the humiliation of her subjection to him. For man and woman alike the term of life's labors is a return to the dust from which they were drawn. Once the sanctions have been declared there is no return for Adam and Eve to their former relationship with Yahweh; the irreversibility of their new status is stressed vividly in their expulsion from the garden: "He drove out the man; and at the east of the garden of Eden he placed the Cherubim, and the flaming sword, which turned every way, to guard the way to the tree of life" (Gn 3:24).

Certainly it is legitimate and even necessary to analyze the paradise story for a greater knowledge of the author's intent; but little is gained by an attempt to delineate details meticulously. Particulars like the location of the garden of Eden or the identity of the four rivers of paradise (Gn 2:10–14) are uncertain, for these are only accessories of the author's portrayal of how life's disorders stem from the original transgression of the first man and woman.

## The progress of sin

Once introduced into the world sin with its consequences advances steadily, and the documentation of the relentless encroachment of evil on Yahweh's creation fills the remaining chapters of the primitive history; thus the progressive human deterioration can be called the principal theme of chs 4–11. The first instance is the murder of Abel, a story which raises almost as many questions as it answers. Is this tribal or personal history? Why was Cain's sacrifice rejected and how did he know that God did not favor him? What was the mark given Cain and what purpose did it serve? Originally the story may have been a tribal history, for Cain was popularly regarded as the eponymous ancestor of the Kenites, people with the same ancestry as Israel but outside the covenant. Furthermore, since the story supposes a rather advanced agricultural civilization and a formal cult, it is not likely that sons of the first man and woman figured in the original version. The story may echo the conflict between two types of civilization—pastoral and agricultural. A similar motif may be the foundation of the struggles between Jacob and Esau in Gn 25–28.

As Yahweh once questioned Adam and his wife so now he addresses Cain: "What have you done? The voice of your brother's blood cries to me from the ground" (Gn 4:10). Punishment follows swiftly: "When you till the soil, it shall not give its fruit to you; a fugitive and a wanderer shall you be on the earth" (4:12). The token which Yahweh placed on Cain is sometimes regarded as a sign of disgrace; from the context however it appears to be a protective mark, perhaps against blood vengeance exacted for fratricide.

Cosmic degeneration is further illustrated in the puzzling narrative of marriages between the sons of God and the daughters of men (Gn 6:1–4). Attempts to render the account more specific by identifying the sons and daughters have not been very successful. At most it is arbitrary to identify the sons of God with the Sethites and the daughters of men with the Kenites. Undoubtedly the sacred writer used mythological stories about the marriage of titans to human women to exemplify the ruthless advance of wickedness throughout the world.

Rebellion, violence, bloodshed—such is the record of mankind from Adam to Noe. As a summary judgment on preceding events and as a prelude to the ensuing story of the Flood the Yahwist reports the Lord's decision: "I will wipe from the earth man whom I have created—man and beast, crawling creature and bird of the air as well—for I regret that I made them" (Gn 6:7).[6] The Flood narrative is interwoven from Yahwist and Priestly traditions, each preserved almost intact with little attempt to suppress discrepancies which arose from the combination of traditions; for example the number of animals in Gn 7:2–3 differs from the number in 6:19–20. The cataclysm described by the Priestly writer is greater in every way; it covers the entire earth and lasts more than a year. Human corruption and Yahweh's judgment on it occupy all the Priestly writer's attention and he is oblivious to the details the Yahwist lingers over. The Priestly author devotes a single brusque verse to reporting the bird sent from the ark (8:7); the Yahwist speaks of several birds and dwells upon the event for seven verses (8:6, 8–12). On occasion however the author of the Priestly account is very detailed; he records the exact measurements of the ark and calculates times and seasons with great care. Behind these minutiae is his conviction of Yahweh's personal activity, which he tries to portray with due theological objectivity.

Modern discoveries of ancient literary materials offer evidence that the story of the Flood in the Bible is but one among many legends of catastrophic inundations. The narrative most resembling the biblical traditions appears in the so-called Flood Tablet (11) of the *Epic of Gilgamesh,* an Akkadian work composed around 2000. The epic was discovered in the library of Ashurbanipal (seventh century) in 1853. Besides the texts in Akkadian other fragmentary recensions testify to the popularity

35

of the work. First published in 1873 when rationalist criticism of the Bible was approaching its zenith, the Babylonian flood story was hailed as the direct model of the biblical narrative; a discrediting of the historicity of the account in Gn soon followed. Specific parallels do exist, but one cannot speak of literary dependence. The stories in both the biblical and the Babylonian texts are based on the same heritage, i.e. memories of one or more severe floods, floods made even more catastrophic by popular tradition. This complex of flood traditions may have been brought from Mesopotamia by the ancestors of the Hebrews, but the biblical story nonetheless has a totally different orientation; it is the vehicle of a religious and moral message quite foreign to the Babylonian version.

A summary of the story in *Gilgamesh* will highlight the chief resemblances and contrasts to the biblical account. A council of the gods decides to destroy the city of Shurrupak. The god Ea warns Utnapishtim, instructing him to build a ship and to take aboard his family and kin as well as the seed of all living things. During the storm and the ensuing flood the frightened gods "cowered like dogs crouched against the outer wall" (11:115). On the seventh day the tempest ceases and the boat comes to rest on Mount Nisir. After another seven days Utnapishtim sends out a dove and then a swallow, both of which return to him; next he sends a raven, which "eats, circles, caws, and turns not round" (11:154). Leaving his boat Utnapishtim offers sacrifice to the gods, who smelled the savor and "crowded like flies about the sacrifice" (11:161). Utnapishtim and his wife are admitted to the assembly of the gods and given a home at the mouth of the rivers.

The biblical Flood story is distinguished from the Babylonian accounts in its presentation of the all-holy Yahweh's righteous judgment on the moral transgressions of his creatures: "The end of all creatures of flesh is in my mind; the earth is full of violence because of them. I will destroy them with the earth" (Gn 6:13).

*Gilgamesh* does not mention any moral causes of the disaster; indeed the action of the gods may be arbitrary and capricious. If Utnapishtim escapes it is not because of his justice but simply because Ea chooses to save him. Like the creation narrative of Gn the biblical story of the Flood may borrow the trappings of myth, but the soul and substance of the biblical accounts owe nothing to mythological concepts.

When Noe returns to dry land his act of sacrifice brings the favor of Yahweh to himself and to all men: "I will never again curse the ground on account of man, for the inclination of man's heart is evil from his youth; I will never again destroy every living creature, as I have done" (Gn 8:21). In this soliloquy Yahweh's reason for sparing man (the evil inclinations of man's heart) is the same as that which prompted his decision to punish man in Gn 6:5ff. The Priestly writer tells of no sacrifice (for in his traditions cultic sacrifice arose in Mosaic times), but he significantly records the blessing given at the new beginning of the world. This benediction, a deliberate evocation of the blessing bestowed upon the first man (see 1:28–29), reinstates mankind to the divine favor with the promises of fertility and a certain dominion over the earth. Not content with blessing Noe Yahweh also makes an alliance with him—the first of the covenants treated by the Priestly writer (9:8–17). The passage is a theological construct enabling the writer to dwell upon his concept of the relation between Yahweh and his people. As a pledge that he will never again destroy all flesh by a flood Yahweh retires his bow of war, placing it in the sky as a perpetual reminder to Noe and his descendants.

## The genealogies

At four points in the primitive history genealogies have been inserted: Gn 4:17ff; 5:1ff; 10:1ff; and 11:10ff. The first two sketch the decendants of Adam as far as Noe; the others the descendants of Noe until Abraham. The Yahwist table in 4:17ff lists the progeny of Adam through Cain but it evinces much greater interest in reporting the progress of civilization than it does in recording genealogical data. The Kenite genealogy is certainly different from the story of Cain and Abel in ch 4, in which Cain is described as a vagabond, not the builder of a city. The genealogy evidently is unaware of the Flood, for it names the sons of Lamech as ancestors of shepherds, musicians and artisans. The parallel Priestly account (5:1ff) follows a strict chronological pattern in tracing Adam's line through Seth: "When Seth was one hundred and five years old, he became the father of Enos. Seth lived eight hundred and seven years after the birth of Enos, and had other sons and daughters. The whole lifetime of Seth was nine hundred and twelve years; then he died" (5:6–8). The key to the Priestly writer's use of numbers is still unknown; thus all attempts to set up an actual historical chronology according to his lists have been futile. The esoteric use of numbers is characteristic of the Semites, as evidenced in the fantastic numbers of the Babylonian King Lists. Similar chronological precision characterizes the Semite genealogy in 11:10ff.

It is sometimes assumed that the Priestly writer's interest in genealogies is merely a pedantic preoccupation with records. Quite the contrary: his concerns are doctrinal or theological and his tables are an effort to arrange the ages of the world and of man theologically. Just as his chronological framework for the creation narrative placed the events he described within the temporal order, so his careful genealogical records deliberately emphasize Yahweh as the Lord of history who deals with his people in definite and irrevocable temporal actions. Even the precision of the chronology, artificial though it may be, is theologically pertinent. The ancients from Adam to Noe have a life span of seven hundred to one thousand years; from Noe to Abraham, two hundred to six hundred years; the patriarchs, one hundred to two hundred years. The Priestly writer does not explain the diminution, but in view of his remarks in Gn 6:11–13 ("The earth was corrupt in the sight of God, and it was filled with violence") the decreasing life span can be considered a subtle commentary on the loss of human vigor as corruption becomes rampant.

The broadened scene of the Table of Nations (Gn 10:1ff) illustrates the fulfillment of Yahweh's blessing of Noe: "Be fruitful and multiply, and fill the earth" (9:1). Here the Priestly writer has organized nations and peoples as descendants of the three sons of Noe: Sem, Ham and Japheth. Ethnic and linguistic relationships do not dictate the grouping, nor are there genuine political ties between the members of a division. Geographic and historical associations seem to explain the alignment; thus the descendants of Japheth compose the northern Peoples of the Sea; Ham's descendants are the men of the southern countries (to which Canaan is joined for historical reasons); and the progeny of Sem are the eastern peoples closely associated with the Hebrews.

It is noteworthy that Israel is not mentioned in the Table of Nations, her derivation from Arphachsad being developed only in Gn 11:10ff. From this fact it is evident that the writer is not concerned to exalt Israel or to contrast her with nations outside the covenant, but rather to testify that the total historical situation (of which Israel forms only a small part) is the creation of Yahweh. The author's ultimate concern of course is to pursue the line of Sem through Arphachsad to Abraham, and he does so in 11:10–32. But if he is thus to narrow his field to a single line why does he elaborate the Table of Nations? His procedure shows that the Priestly writer was aware of the mystery of divine election and wanted to make it theologically vivid by contrasting Israel with the other people who were equally the creation of Yahweh, but who were not the object of special predilection.

## The conclusion of primitive history

The recital of man's irreversible deterioration reaches its terminus in the story of the Tower of Babel, which concludes the pre-history. The narrative speaks of two distinct constructions: the building of a city and of a lofty tower or ziggurat. The reference to Babel at the conclusion of the story suggests that the tower—like the 270-foot ziggurat of Etemenanki dedicated to Marduk, protector of Babylon—was a shrine to a heathen deity. The writer does not specify the nature of man's offense. That the building involved rebellion against Yahweh is not stated directly, but the Hebrew connotation of the word "Babel" indicates that such defection is implied. Pride is likewise implicit in the builders' exhortaton: "Let us make a name for ourselves lest we be scattered all over the earth" (Gn 11:4), as well as in Yahweh's decision to curb their presumptuous aspirations: "This is the beginning of what they will do. Hereafter they will not be restrained from anything which they determine to do" (11:6).

Interrupting the work in progress Yahweh confused (*balal*) the builders' speech and scattered them over the earth. Two etiologies, perhaps the original point of the earlier traditions, are thus still retained: the origin of various languages and a popular etymology of Babel, which actually means gate of God. The etiologies however are only incidental to the dominant interest: the portrayal of man's arrogant attempt to usurp divine prerogatives. The bold anthropomorphism of Yahweh's concern over the tower and his investigation of the work are not reminiscent of a mythic struggle between titans and the gods; in fact there is no extant extrabiblical parallel to this story. The picture furnishes an ironic contrast between puny human efforts and the calm, majestic action of Yahweh. Men lay their solicitous plans: "Let us make bricks and bake them. . . . Let us build. . . . Let us make a name. . . ;" but Yahweh with a single decision brings all their plans to nought: "Let us go down, and there confuse their language" (Gn 11:3–7).

The gloomy scene of mankind confounded at the Tower of Babel closes the primitive history. The dismal conclusion departs from the pattern in the preceding accounts whereby sin made ever more devastating progress in the world which God had created good. Adam's initial deviation from the divine will incurred dire sanctions but the harsh situation was mitigated by Yahweh's fatherly solicitude: "The Lord God made garments of skin for Adam and his wife and clothed them" (Gn 3:21). Likewise the Lord punished the murderer Cain, yet at the same time afforded him a protective mark as he wandered restless through the earth (4:15). Then after the Flood Yahweh renewed the blessing first bestowed upon Adam: "Be fruitful and multiply, and fill the earth" (9:1).

Despite so many fresh starts men repeated the wretched pattern of rebellion and violence until finally the Lord confused their speech and scattered them over the earth (Gn 11:7–8). The story marks a point of no return in man's relations to God. Cut off from the Lord, men find themselves separated from their brethren as well. On this note the story ends; no compassionate utterance of the Lord, no promise of rescue intrudes a vestige of hope. The sacred writer has completed his account of man's progressive perversion and he is at the end also of his assurances that the Lord, despite man's wickness, has not cast off his creatures utterly. The dry statements of the genealogy which follows (11:10–32) underline the bleakness of affairs for which no happy denouement seems possible.

## The patriarchal history

Precisely at this point, the nadir of man's relations to God, the salvation history introduces a new approach of God to man in the choice of Abraham as the father of a chosen people. Like a seed the salvific plan lies hidden within the catalogue of Sem's descendants: "Thare was the father of Abram, Nahor, and Aran" (Gn 11:27); but who could suspect that this laconic report is prelude to the grandeur to be unfolded in the promises?

The rise of Israel as a people rests historically on the union of her tribes in the worship of Yahweh, a fact upon which all later Hebrew history is built. Paradoxically however our understanding of how Israel evolved into an historical reality is based on pretribal traditions whose contents, though admittedly of decisive importance, presuppose the subsequent history of Israel. The primitive cultic credo of Dt 26:5ff summarizes one of these traditions: "My father was a wandering Aramean who went down to Egypt with a small household and lived there as an alien. But there he became a nation great, strong and numerous." Other similar traditions, expanded and unified, compose the patriarchal history of Gn. In their earliest forms these traditions were oral, localized reminiscences of family forebears or etiologies of names and customs which were amalgamated after a protracted process of modification that cannot now be traced in detail. In their definitive version in the Pentateuch the patriarchal adventures have been incorporated into a broad theme recording how Israel's ancestors under divine guidance migrated from northwest Mesopotamia, entered the land of Canaan and there lived as resident strangers while awaiting the possession of the land promised them by divine favor. The memory she preserved of her beginnings testifies that the Lord of the world marked Israel as the vehicle through which all peoples of the earth would be blessed.

That this testimony exists is itself an historical fact and hence part of the history of Israel. But the degree to which the traditions witnessed by the testimony can be used to reconstruct historical events is debatable. True, the historicity of the patriarchal accounts is not a direct concern of the critic in his task of showing how the traditions were linked to Israel's consciousness of her relation to Yahweh; nonetheless the biblicist must inevitably come to grips with the problem of the relationship between history as presented in the patriarchal narratives and the religion in whose service the traditions are employed. This encounter is necessary because the reconstruction of the history and faith of early Israel affects the interpretation of later Israelite history and of the Old Testament as a whole.

The first problem concerning the historicity of the patriarchal traditions stems from the lack of contemporary records of the period. Working on the principle that ancient narratives are primarily sources for the period in which they were written, not for the times they report, many proponents of the documentary theory refused to acknowledge the historical worth of traditions referring to remote ages. Reinforced by the theory of evolutionary religious development their view quickly reduced patriarchal religion to a projection of later Yahwism; and to explain the presence of the patriarchs in the traditions they had recourse to theories more ingenious than satisfying. Critics like Wellhausen failed to realize that the writing of a tradition marks the end of an era, not the beginning. Although the dates assigned to a document may be accurate they give no clue to the age of the traditions described in the document.

As we have already noted, archeological discoveries have altered the harsh view prevalent in the last century, and thousands of texts contemporaneous with the period of Israel's beginnings have supplied a frame of reference for the historical evaluation of biblical traditions. In no instance has the new evidence submitted "proof" of a single event in the patriarchal stories; yet by furnishing many parallels and by corroboration of countless details it has shown that the narratives must be taken seriously as an exact portrait of institutions and customs in the patriarchal period, and hence that they reflect a valid memory of the past.[7] Despite the presumption of authenticity thus attached to the patriarchal traditions not all scholars concede that the biblical narratives are reliable sources of history. Martin Noth, possibly the most influential of these critics, agrees that the Pentateuch as a coalescence of sacred traditions does contain historical information, but he denies that the Books of Moses can be accepted as a coherent historical narrative. Just how far the Pentateuch can be taken as a source for Israelite history is a problem to be solved only by an examination of each separate unit of tradition, i.e. by a construction of a history of the traditions. Noth values the contribution made by extrabiblical remains to Israel's history, and he does not completely dismiss the worth of archeological discoveries; but he insists that their witness is after all indirect and therefore incapable of establishing the historical accuracy of the narratives. His negative evaluation of the historical elements in Israelite traditions leaves unanswered the question of Israel's origin and offers no adequate explanation of her faith.

Gerhard von Rad shares Noth's views to some extent but his work is distinguished by decidedly theological interests. Whereas Noth stresses the impossibility of determining historical content von Rad emphasizes the irrelevancy of such determination. An historical kernel is found, to be sure, in many of the stories but the genuine historical concern is always Yahweh's dealings with his people. Accordingly, says von Rad, the faith of the Hebrews must be explained in terms of what Israel thought of her relation to Yahweh, not by the results of modern studies on Israel's actual bearing to her neighbors or by historical facts.

While agreeing with Noth that history properly so called is not available in the Pentateuchal records, critics like William F. Albright and John Bright are more sanguine in their appraisal of the patriarchal narratives as dependable sources for Israelite history. If the writing of Israelite history is not be be completely nihilistic, they assert, one must examine the traditions against the world of their day, and in this light draw whatever conclusions the evidence allows. In the reconstruction of Hebrew history the distinction between the empiric methodology of Albright and the tradition-history of Noth is becoming ever more acute.[8]

## The promises

One of the earliest and most perduring of the traditions comprising the heritage of Israel is that of the promises made to the patriarchs. Events at Babel indicated that the relationship between Yahweh and his creatures was at an end; must man now continue to live severed from the Lord? The onset of salvation history with the call of Abraham answers the question:

> Leave your country, your kinsfolk, and your father's house,
> for the land which I will show you;
> I will make a great nation of you.
> I will bless you and make your name great,
> so that you shall be a blessing.
> I will bless them that bless you,
> and curse them that curse you.
> In you shall all the nations of the earth be blessed (Gn 12:1–3).

The command of leaving home and family is attached to two promises: a new land and a great posterity. Today numerous progeny is still regarded as a great blessing, a special mark of divine favor among peoples of the East; and to nomads and seminomads sown land with its abundance of food and its stable life is an inestimable good. The double theme of land and children here introduced for the first time echoes again and again throughout the pages of Gn. Although individual traditions emphasize now the one, now the other aspect the two ideas are rarely separated in passages which directly report the conference of the divine pledges. In only two instances is the promise of posterity given apart from the promise of the land in Gn: the promise of a child to Sara (18:10) and the promise of descendants to Isaac (26:24). Seven times the assurances of Gn 12:1–3 are repeated to Abraham: 12:7; 13:14–17; 15:5–7, 18; 17:4–8; 18:10; and 22:17–18. The promises are renewed for Isaac in 26:2–5 and again in 26:24. At various times Jacob also receives a reiteration of Yahweh's intent to give him land and posterity: 28:13–15; 35:9–12; and 46:3–4. Besides these direct reports of the bestowal and renewal of the promises there are frequent indirect references to one or both of them: 24:7; 28:3–4; 32:13; 48:4; and 50:24.

## The promise as covenant

In calling Abraham, Yahweh seemingly narrowed the field of his redemptive operations. The blessing of Noe carried an injunction to multiply and fill the earth (Gn 9:1); the promise to Abraham particularizes the blessing: it is Abraham's progeny which will become a great nation. "In you shall all the nations of the earth be blessed" admits of several interpretations. A possible translation is: "May you be blessed as Abraham was," a grammatically more exact rendering than the usual translation which appears in the Septuagint and which has been canonized by use in Acts 3:25 and Gal 3:8. So considered the benediction pronounced on Abraham will pass into proverb as the epitome of all a nation can hope for and his blessing will be a model for every benediction they invoke upon themselves. But besides having this reflexive meaning the verb can also be construed passively; hence it is through Abraham that all nations will participate in the divine blessings; through Abraham as mediator Yahweh's plan of salvation will be effected throughout the world. The first of the promises is somewhat vague: the territory pledged to Abraham is referred to only as "the land which I will show you." Moreover, except for the notation "Now Sarai was barren" in the genealogy (Gn 11:30), no hint is given of the difficulties which will impede the fulfillment of the promise of progeny.

The most solemn enunciations of the promises occur in Gn 15 and 17 where Yahweh binds himself by covenant to their fulfillment. In the account of Gn 12:1ff Abraham's response to God's pronouncements was evident only in the obedience he rendered, but in ch 15 his more immediate reactions are noted. As it now stands the chapter is a skillful blend of two traditions, roughly delineated by the sections 1–6 (E) and 7–18 (J). The promises of vv 1–6 center in the progeny, those of vv 7–18, the land. When the puzzled Abraham remonstrates: "To me you have given no descendants; the slave born in my house will be my heir," Yahweh reassures him: "He shall not be your heir; your heir shall be one of your own flesh" (15:3–4). Again Abraham queries: "O Lord God, how am I to know that I shall possess it [the land]?" (15:8). Yahweh replies with directions for the covenantal ceremonies described in vv 9–11 and 17. The rites of cutting the victims in two and of the transporting of the smoking oven and fiery torch through the lane between the halves are very mysterious, although they may be cultic actions familiar to the hearers. Aside from his preparation of the victims Abraham is passive: "As the sun was setting, Abram fell into a deep sleep; and terror came upon him, a great darkness" (15:12). Nor is the relation of Yahweh to the phenomenon elaborated. In any event the gist of the narrative conveys Yahweh's solemn commitment to his pledge: "To your posterity I will give this land" (15:18).

The Priestly writer also has an account of a covenant with Abraham, an account vastly different however from the more

47

primitive narrative of ch 15. The characteristic promises are imbedded in a heavy, verbose, theological passage which pays scant attention to the patriarch's reactions except to note that "Abram fell prostrate" (Gn 17:3). The repetitions throughout Yahweh's speech indicate that several Priestly traditions have been joined; the total effect is somewhat ponderous and makes of Abraham a mere lay figure against which to arrange theological considerations. Heretofore Yahweh had exacted nothing from Abraham beyond faith and obedience to the command to leave his home, but in the covenant of ch 17 he imposed the obligation of circumcision for the patriarch and his descendants. The fully developed legislative details on the ceremony of circumcision suggest a late period for this passage. Although circumcision was no doubt practiced in early times it was not a distinctively Israelite custom nor was it legislated in the principal biblical corpora. The Priestly writer himself does not refer to it outside Gn 17 except in Ex 12:44 and Lv 12:3. Other references to circumcision do not speak of it as a rite imposed by divine command. Only after the Exile did circumcision become the distinctive sign of allegiance to Yahweh and the covenant. To gain authority and prestige for the postexilic observance the Priestly writer in ch 17 sought to establish circumcision as a primitive obligation imposed by Yahweh as a token of the covenant.

The usual terminology for covenant making, *karat b*e*rît,* to cut a covenant, is not employed by the Priestly writer; he uses instead *qum b*e*rît,* to establish a covenant (17:7) or *natan b*e*rît,* to give a covenant (17:2). The deliberate change of vocabulary is significant. The ordinary term was used in covenants initiated by the free will of both participants; Yahweh's covenant however involves no exchange between equals. Rather it is a gratuitous bestowal of divine favor quite beyond the power of man to achieve for himself. If the covenant exists at all it is only because Yahweh has chosen to establish it, not because man has entered into negotiations for it.

## Obstacles to the promise

Once he is aware of the divine will in his regard Abraham sets out to fulfill it. Considering the close ties between tribal members the command to leave country and kinsfolk is no small thing. So intent is the sacred writer upon the promises however that he shows no interest in the patriarch's migration from Haran to Canaan. Suddenly Abraham appears in Sichem (Gn 12:6), where the promise of land is further specified by Yahweh's declaration: "To your descendants I will give this land" (12:7). But even as Abraham pitches his tent near Bethel and thinks, perhaps, that he is at journey's end there comes the first indication that the twofold pledge will not be readily attained. Because of famine Abraham is forced to move south to Egypt; there he jeopardizes the future mother of the promised child by pretending Sara is his sister and letting her be taken into the royal harem. Since marriage was not basically monogamous a man could have intercourse with women of his own household, such as slaves or prisoners. Adultery strictly so called however was always severely punished; hence if Abraham was known as the husband of Sara he would in all probability have been killed before Sara was taken by Pharao. Yahweh will not permit Abraham's careless and cowardly behavior to void his promise; rather "the Lord struck Pharao and his household with great plagues because of Sarai, Abram's wife" (12:17). Pharao had acted in good faith, yet he was punished. The statement reflects the biblical theory which judges primarily on the basis of the act itself and pays little heed to the agent's conscious intention or state of soul. On discovering the true situation Pharao rebuked Abraham and summarily dismissed him.

Twice the same motif of threat to the child of promise recurs: once involving Abraham and Sara at Gerara (Gn 20:1–18 [E]) and a second time concerning Isaac and Rebecca at Gerara (26:6–11 [J]). The facts in both these accounts closely resemble those of Gn 12:10–16, but there are differences in tone and emphasis between the three versions. The story of Isaac and Rebecca is the simplest and perhaps the earliest of the three; subsequently the narrative was developed, given a new setting and assigned different characters. As the Elohist handles the story (20:1–18) the dominant motif of threat to the mother of the promised child has been glossed over by preoccupation with the question of guilt. The writer is at pains to justify Abimelech (20:4–6) and to exonerate Abraham by noting that Sara is really his half sister. (Marriage with a half sister was permitted according to 2 Sm 13:13. The later legislation of Lv 18:9, 11 and Dt 27:22 forbade it.) The vindication of Abimelech is readily appreciated but the defense of Abraham creates a certain tension: why should the man who regards God's promise so cheaply be made intercessor for the innocent king? (Gn 20:7, 17). The incident may reflect a later tradition of Abraham as intercessor (see also 19:29); at the same time it underscores that Yahweh is beholden to no one and bestows his favors where he will. The Yahwist on the contrary prunes away all superfluous details, even those in which the reader, at least the modern reader, is vitally interested. What leads Pharao, for instance, to connect the plagues with the presence of Sara in his harem? The reader also looks, but vainly, for some moral reflection on the disagreeable situation. The events are simply allowed to speak for themselves.

Yahweh's power has protected Abraham's wife, but to what avail? Sara is barren. Abraham's lament: "I am childless. . . . To me you have given no descendants" (Gn 15:2–3) continues the ever-present theme: how is the promise of posterity to be kept? Sara herself took a hand in promoting the divine plan by human contrivance (ch 16). Following a custom evidenced in the Nuzu tablets she bade Abraham: "Go in to my maid; perhaps I shall get children through her" (16:2). Abraham's feelings in the matter are not revealed. Did he too think to advance God's designs by human means? When the slave maid Agar conceived by Abraham she viewed her mistress with contempt and thus gave Sara the legal right to humiliate her. (The Code of Hammurabi has a similar provision.) The humiliation imposed by Sara caused the pregnant Agar to flee southward to the desert; there an angel of the Lord appeared to her, assured her a great posterity and bade her return to Sara (16:9–10).

The controversial figure of the angel of the Lord, *mal'akh YHWH,* is here introduced for the first time. In its most probable derivation *mal'akh* signifies messenger, though translated through the Greek as angel. The actions and words of the messenger frequently suggest however that the *mal'akh YHWH* is to be identified with the Lord himself. In the present story for example vv 7, 9 and 10 specify that the *mal'akh YHWH* spoke to Agar; yet in v 13 (which is the point of the narrative etiologically considered) Agar "named the Lord, who spoke to her: 'You are the God of vision;' for she said, 'Have I really seen God and remained alive after my vision?' " The same discrepancy occurs in the variant of the Agar story, Gn 21:17–18. Similar use of the term is found throughout the patriarchal history: 22:11 (the sacrifice of Isaac); 31:11–13 (Jacob recounting his labors for Laban); and 48:16 (Jacob's blessing of Joseph's sons). The phrase is also employed elsewhere in the Pentateuch, especially in Ex and Nm. The same puzzling ambivalence between Yahweh and his angel is also found in Gn 18 and 32:22–31, although in these places the particular phrase *mal'akh YHWH* is not used.

Such consistent dichotomy must be deliberate. One explanation is that the angel is an addition to primitive traditions in which Yahweh himself was the agent; the insertion of the messenger was the result of theological reflection which, through reverence for the divine transcendence, blurred the immediacy of man's relation to God by intruding a mediating figure who still spoke the direct words of Yahweh. Other critics hold that the messenger was the original figure in these passages. By analyses of texts and comparisons with usage in Babylonian and Egyptian literature they would prove that Yahwism, having reduced the original role of the messenger or vizier of God, inserted the direct action of Yahweh into passages where the messengers appear.

The Elohist version of the Agar story places the event after the birth of Ishmael and Isaac. This presentation of the double tradition as two separate occurrences, one before and one after the birth of Ishmael, has created chronological difficulties since the stories were inserted into the Priestly traditions without any consistent effort to harmonize them. According to Gn 16:16 and 21:5 Ishmael must have been nearly seventeen years old at the time of the second expulsion. The discord was not lost upon the ancient scribes, who evidently manipulated the text (e.g. v 14) to tone down the jarring effect.

The two accounts display marked differences in spirit and emphasis. The Yahwist does not seek to enlist the reader's sympathy in any particular direction. He carefully avoids revealing his own views and furnishes no clue to Abraham's feelings beyond the simple statement: "Abram listened to Sarai. . . . 'The maid is in your power; do to her what seems good to you'" (Gn 16:3–6). Agar's adventure in the desert is related with such paucity of detail that one is scarcely aware of her suffering. How different the Elohist narrative is. Sympathy for Agar is first aroused by Sara's petty complaints about her (21:9–10). That sympathy is increased as the details of the expulsion unfold: the wandering, the thirst, the mother's pain at the prospect of the child's death (21:14–16). Abraham's feelings are also spelled out: "The matter was very distressing to Abraham on account of his son" (21:12); and the writer carefully excuses him from any blame in the heartless action. It may also be noted that the Yahwist stresses the etiology of Beer–lahai–roi (16:13–14); whereas the Elohist only mentions the well with no reference to its name.

Both stories however stress Ishmael's future as the father of a mighty nation; far from minimizing the pledges given Abraham for the child of promise, the blessings accorded Ishmael are a foil to the still more lavish gifts reserved for Isaac. The angel depicts Ishmael as a fitting ancestor for the proud Bedouin: "He shall be a wild ass of a man, his hand against everyone, and everyone's hand against him; he shall dwell apart, opposing all his kinsmen" (Gn 16:12). This description may have formed part of an early tradition about the Ishmaelites; later it was added to the more fully developed Abraham cycle. Legends about Ishmael's later life are preserved in 21:21 and 25:9, 12–18.

The tribal history and the etiology in the Agar narrative should not obscure the central point: Yahweh's plans do not require human prudence and ingenuity for their advancement, nor do human estimations of what is right and fitting sway the Lord in his unhampered distribution of divine favors. The Priestly writer reinforces the element of gratuity as he relates how Abraham implores Yahweh: "Oh, that Ishmael may live in your favor!" (Gn 17:18), to which the Lord answers: "No, but Sara your wife will bear you a son, and you shall call him Isaac. I will establish my covenant with him as a perpetual covenant for his descendants after him" (17:19). And again: "As for Ishmael, I have heard you. I will bless him, . . . but my covenant I will establish with Isaac" (17:20). The promises do not preclude divine favors to other nations—the Ishmaelites too are the object of blessing—but the promises Yahweh has reserved for the people peculiarly his own.

## Advance of the promise

Clearly it is not through Ishmael that Yahweh will make of Abraham a great nation. But the manifestation of the divine will in Ishmael's regard makes no positive contribution to the accomplishment of the promise, for Sara is now both barren and old; how can a child come from her? The Yahwist answers by posing a query: "Is anything too wonderful for the Lord?" (Gn 18:14). Heretofore the promises had spoken in general terms of descendants and posterity, or in poetic fashion of progeny like the stars of heaven or the sands of the sea shore. Now Yahweh moves to the concrete fulfillment of the promise in terms of a particular child, Abraham's son to be born of Sara within a year. While visiting the patriarch and his wife, Yahweh makes the astounding announcement: "I will surely return to you at this time next year . . . and Sara your wife shall have a son" (18:10). How Abraham received this statement is not recorded but the realistic Sara, listening inside the tent door, greeted the announcement with laughter. Her mirth was soon stifled by the visitor's uncanny question: "Why did Sara laugh? . . . Is anything too wonderful for the Lord?" (18:13–14). With keen insight the narrator describes Sara's confusion: "But Sara denied it, saying, 'I did not laugh'; for she was afraid" (18:15). The scene closes with Yahweh's firm and categoric utterance: "You did laugh" (18:15).

Finally, after long years marked by gracious renewal of the promises, by careless disregard of Yahweh's pledges or by faltering efforts to achieve them by human expedients, the birth of the child is announced in very simple terms: "The Lord looked after Sara as he had said; the Lord did to Sara as he had promised" (Gn 21:1–2). All the anxious hopes of Gn 12–21 come to their fulfillment in the birth of Isaac.[9] The arrival of the child however is not simply a happy ending to the isolated recital of trials and tests imposed on Abraham; it is an event which carries the salvation history forward into a new phase directed to the achievement of Yahweh's more comprehensive designs. The birth of Isaac is a stage, not the final goal of Yahweh's plan.

Accordingly it is no surprise that soon the inscrutable ways of Yahweh are again operative in a manner which seems to threaten the very gifts he had bestowed: Abraham is commanded to travel to the district of Moria (traditionally regarded as the site of the city of Jerusalem) and there sacrifice his beloved son, all the dearer because he was so long awaited (Gn 22). What greater renunciation can be asked of a father than the death of his son? But the command to sacrifice the promised child also imposes an excruciating test on Abraham's faith in the Lord through whose favor Isaac had been given. The patriarch had not importuned Yahweh for his gifts; the promises were not so much objects of Abraham's desires as free pledges from the Lord. Quite unexpectedly the words had burst upon his startled ear: "I will make a great nation of you" (12:2). And Abraham had believed. All the more shocking then is Yahweh's seeming determination to bring to ruin what he had proposed so gratuitously. Before his birth Isaac had been the object of divine predilection and solicitude. Will Yahweh now make void his promise? The Elohist lingers over the aspects calculated to bring out the heart-rending nature of the demand: "Take your only son Isaac whom you love and go into the district of Moria, and there offer him as a holocaust on the hill which I shall point out to you" (22:2). Abraham's inner emotions are depicted with marked restraint but the graphic particulars of his actions provide an appropriate background for his somber thoughts which, though unexpressed, pulse through the scene.

55

The structure of vv 7 and 8 is particularly effective, with the slow question and answer set to the rhythm of the travelers' footsteps as they inexorably approach the moment of sacrifice.

Although the sacrifice of Isaac may have been a cultic saga justifying the substitution of animal for human sacrifice, such a concept is quite foreign to the narrative as it is preserved in the Pentateuch. The material was in constant flux up to the time of its final redaction and is therefore open to many meanings. The etiological emphasis of the earlier traditions was lost as other elements assumed greater importance, so that the name Yahweh-yireh (the Lord sees or the Lord provides) is a minor note, not being the name of a prominent cultic center. The structure of the pericope tones down the horror of child sacrifice and by concentrating on Abraham's actions points to the test of his obedience as the essence of the story. Earlier his trust and faith had been tried by delay in the fulfillment of the promise; at Moria his faith was scrutinized even more searchingly as Yahweh, in seeming contradiction to all previous assurances, demanded the sacrifice of Isaac. To crown Abraham's obedience Yahweh repeats and expands the promises: like the stars of heaven will his progeny be and his descendants will possess the gates of their enemies (Gn 22:17). When the promises were first revealed, and before Abraham could prove his obedience, Yahweh had declared: "In you shall all nations of the earth be blessed" (12:3). Now that the patriarch has passed through the fire of obedience this assurance resounds more significantly: "In your descendants all the nations of the earth shall be blessed, because you have obeyed me" (22:18).

## The promise of the land

Posterity and land of his own—these are Abraham's portion from the Lord. The traditions of Gn 12–22 are so centered in future offspring however that the promise of land remains in the background. Indirectly the subject was broached early in the cycle by a story contrasting the behavior of Abraham and Lot as they prepared to separate from one another (Gn 13).[10] Availing himself of Abraham's magnanimity Lot took the fertile, well-watered section of the land, "like the Lord's garden, or like Egypt" (13:10); nonetheless Abraham's is the better portion, for he let Yahweh choose for him. Lot's territory lay on the left, Abraham's on the right. Such a designation was an immediate clue to the Hebrew listener, who proverbially regarded the right as the favorable side and the left as the unlucky one. The writer inserts an additional subtle reminder of the disastrous consequences of Lot's supposedly felicitous choice: "Now the men of Sodom were wicked, and sinned exceedingly against the Lord" (13:13). Abraham's generosity and trust bring a renewal of the promise, this time elaborated and dramatically expressed: "Raise your eyes, and from where you are now look to the north and the south and the east and the west. All the land which you see I will give to you and your posterity forever" (13:14–15).

Failure to attain permanent possession of the territory apportioned to him posed no less a trial to Abraham's faith than did obstacles to the birth of the promised child. Despite years of residence in Canaan no portion of the land was his own; always he had dwelt as a *ger,* a resident stranger. Was he to die without entering into the possession assured him by Yahweh? The Priestly writer answers this question by relating Abraham's purchase of burial ground for his beloved Sara (Gn 23). Why should the writer who is generally satisfied to condense and abbreviate narrative sections here expatiate on Abraham's purchase of the field of Machphela? The reason is that the purchase, even though a mere business transaction, actually marks the initial step in the acquisition of the promised land and hence has a vital connection with the faith of Abraham—and of Israel. At first Abraham bargains only for the cave at the end of the field, but he ends by purchasing the entire piece of land. The Priestly narrator does not indicate the significance of the transaction; nonetheless his emphasis upon the transfer of the land and its location leaves no doubt that the full import of the deed is clear to him:

Thus Ephron's field in Machphela, facing Mamre, that is, the field, the cave and all the trees in the entire field, became the property of Abraham in the presence of all the Hethites, his fellow citizens. After this Abraham buried his wife Sara in the cave of the field at Machphela, facing Mamre, that is Hebron, in the land of Chanaan. Thus the field with its cave passed from the Hethites to Abraham for use as a burial ground (Gn 23: 17–20).

We have already noted that there is close correspondence between customs described in the patriarchal narratives and those known from extrabiblical sources. Abraham's purchase of Machphela is a case in point, for a Hittite law imposes feudal dues upon the man in whose name an entire piece of property is held. The provision clarifies Abraham's insistence on buying the cave alone and the Hittites' insistence on selling him the whole field. The intimate knowledge of the subtleties of Hittite law and custom, which fell into disuse about 1200, attests the antiquity of the tradition behind the story.[11]

Machphela was not the resting place for Sara alone; when Abraham was gathered to his kinsmen he was laid beside his wife (Gn 25:10). Isaac too, although he lived as a stranger in Canaan, was buried in Machphela, the one portion of land he possessed. Jacob's final request of Joseph is for burial with his fathers "in the cave which is in the field of Ephron, the Hethite, the cave in the field of Machphela, facing Mamre in the land of Chanaan" (49:29–30). Thus in Machphela the patriarchs

58

owned some small part of the promised land and at least in death they entered into their possession.[12]

## The promise in the life of Isaac

After the climactic birth and sacrifice of Isaac the biblical narrative levels off to a more leisurely, less dramatic phase as it records the advance of the promises in the lives of Isaac and Jacob. How tenaciously Abraham clung to the assurance that Canaan would belong to his descendants is evident in the plans he makes for Isaac's marriage. Although desirous that his son should marry one of his own kindred Abraham insists that Isaac must not return to the former home in northwest Mesopotamia: Aram Naharaim, the land of the two rivers. Solemnly he admonishes his servant:

> Never take my son back there. The Lord, the God of heaven, who took me from my father's house, from the land of my kindred, who spoke to me and swore to me, 'I will give this land to your descendants,' will send his angel ahead of you and you will obtain a wife for my son there. If the woman does not wish to follow you, you will be released from this oath; but do not take my son back there (Gn 24:6–8).

The chronicle of the servant's efforts at matchmaking shows a texture different from that of the preceding narratives; it is more unified in structure and more secular in tone. Eliezer's discharge of his commission is related in a manner perhaps too repetitive for modern tastes, for example in Gn 24:34–49 when all the events of 24:1–23 are leisurely reviewed in the message to Laban and his family. Such treatment needs no justification other than the literary tastes of the writer and his readers; in addition a savoring of the details helps illustrate how Yahweh has providentially brought the mission to a successful completion, as both Eliezer and Laban point out (vv 27, 48, 50).

Once the marriage has been arranged and Rebecca has consented to accompany Eliezer back to Canaan the continuation of Abraham's line seems assured. The story then moves along brusquely with a minimum of detail: "So the servant took Rebecca and departed. . . . The servant told Isaac all that he had done. Isaac led Rebecca into the tent and took her to wife" (Gn 24:61, 66–67). A disconcerting genealogy has been inserted at this point—disconcerting because the recital of Abraham's children by another wife, Cetura, detracts from the uniqueness of the promised child and weakens the theme of promise and fulfillment. The list cannot be explained by the Priestly writer's penchant for genealogies since Gn 25:1–6 is usually attributed to the Yahwist.

The contrasts between the patriarchs raise the question: what was the original relationship of the patriarchs to one another? Gn 12–50 describes Abraham, Isaac and Jacob as father, son and grandson, but perhaps this relationship is a supplement to primitive traditions. It is generally agreed that the narratives grew from local legends of family ancestors; the localization of the Abraham-Isaac stories in southern Palestine and those of Jacob in central Palestine and the land east of the Jordan tends to verify this assumption. Quite possibly then the persons described as father, son and grandson originally had no connection with one another. As stories from one region began to circulate in other sections there was an inevitable revision of details and reassignment of roles. Certain aspects of the traditions were dropped; still others were developed or duplicated; and some figures emerged at the expense of other characters. In contrast to Abraham and Jacob, the patriarch Isaac is a shadowy figure; indeed whatever color glows in his life is reflected through Abraham or Jacob. Although on two different occasions Yahweh renews the original pledges (Gn 26:2–5 and 23–25) the absence of conflict and opposition lessens interest in the promises. A passing reference to the barrenness of Rebecca

(25:21) does revive the problem of how the promise is to be fulfilled, but the difficulty immediately fades away when Rebecca conceives in answer to Isaac's prayer. And since Rebecca's danger in the royal harem at Gerara (26:6–11) occurs after the birth of Esau and Jacob, the incident creates no problem for the attainment of the promise and hence rouses less concern than it did in the other versions. Not until the conflict between Esau and Jacob, first over the birthright and then over the blessing, does the subject of the promise come alive once again and suggest fresh problems.

### The promise in the life of Jacob

In the Jacob chronicle the sacred writer stresses yet another aspect of the relation between the divine promises and human activity: can Yahweh's plans evolve despite man's machinations; can Yahweh incorporate into his designs faulty—that is, guilty —human acts? When Sara tried to secure offspring for Abraham through Agar (Gn 16:1 ff) Yahweh rejected her help, but his action on this occasion does not tell the whole story. On the one hand Yahweh can dispense with human activity in achieving his goal (thesis of the Abraham cycle); on the other he may, if he so chooses, utilize man's help, turning to his own ends even human malice (thesis of the Jacob cycle).

To develop his topic the sacred writer has made use of popular traditions for his own purposes. Recollections of a wily, calculating ancestor were a source of delight to the clever man's descendants, the more so if the persons outwitted were themselves forebears of the descendants' enemies. Thus Esau through additions to the primitive traditions is portrayed in contemptuous terms as the father of the hated Edomites. He is described as red (*admônî*) and hairy (*śē'ār*)—references to the location of

61

Edom (*'edôm*) in the south (*sē'îr*). The play on words is repeated in Gn 25:30. Early versions of the story possibly played up the opposition between hunting and pastoral life. Esau is shown as a nomadic hunter, "a man of the open country;" Jacob is "a settled man who stayed among the tents" (25:27). While retaining their robust secular character the adventures of the nimble-witted Jacob were diverted to support the premise that Yahweh can write straight with crooked lines. So subtly is the point made that it can be easily missed by the reader, distracted by his effort to justify what is at best questionable behavior on the part of Jacob, Rebecca, et al.

Born grasping his brother's heel, even at birth Jacob merited his name of supplanter (Gn 25:23–26). Later he took advantage of Esau's carelessness and greed to get for himself the elder's birthright (25:29–34). These events are preludes to his calculated usurpation of the firstborn's blessing, whereby the promises were diverted to Jacob (Gn 27). The multiplicity of details builds up suspense until the moment when Isaac, convinced that Esau was standing before him, imparted his final benediction. To the Hebrews a blessing was an ontological reality having an existence in some way independent of the one conferring it; once given it could not be revoked.[13] Knowing this, Esau cried out in anguish: "He took my birthright (*bᵉkōrâh*) and now he has taken my blessing (*bᵉrākâh*)" (27:36). Now Isaac has exhausted his blessing with the bestowal of fertility and dominion upon Jacob: "God give you dew from heaven, and fruitfulness of the earth, abundance of grain and wine. Let nations serve you, peoples bow down to you. Be master of your brothers; may your mother's sons bow down to you" (27:28–29). Moved by Esau's pleading Isaac can only repeat to him a formula which, despite its external resemblance to the blessing accorded Jacob, stresses that the full force of the paternal benediction has been expended on the younger son:

"Without the fruitfulness of the earth shall your dwelling be; without the dew of heaven above" (27:39).

The trickery of Rebecca and her son has constantly scandalized exegetes. Augustine was not the last to worry about the guilt of the bearer of the promise; his uneasy decision that the deceit of Jacob and Rebecca constituted "non mendacium, sed mysterium" has been echoed in subsequent efforts to palliate their action. Surely there is a mystery but it is not the lie; the true mystery is the inscrutable ways of the Lord, who directs even the wickedness of his creatures to his own ends. Jacob, not Esau, was to be the beneficiary of the divine promises first made to Abraham: such was Yahweh's decree. All things are in his hands and so completely is he master of the situation that he can accomplish his designs even through the perverted ways of men.

Jacob is now the man of the promise; to him accordingly the pledges are renewed. Since Esau bore a grudge—not unnaturally —because of the stolen blessing, Jacob fled to his uncle Laban in Aram Naharaim. Resting one night enroute Jacob was granted a dream and a theophany (Gn 28:10–22), perhaps two distinct experiences, which the narrator combined with indifferent success. Yahweh revealed himself as "the God of Abraham your father, and the God of Isaac" (28:13) and in language reminiscent of the promises to Abraham renewed the guarantee that a numerous posterity would own the land on which Jacob lay.

The initial manifestation of the Lord's favor is followed by Jacob's twenty-year sojourn in Aram Naharaim, during which time little is heard of the promises. The battle of wits between the shrewd patriarch and his grasping father-in-law, the rivalry between Rachel and Lia, the growth of Jacob's family—all these are secular both in subject and in treatment. The relation of the material to the theme of the promise appears nebulous until one remembers that these are the family traditions of the

Israelite tribes among whom the patriarchal promises were so abundantly fulfilled. An appreciative audience never tired of hearing the family sagas of how Jacob the supplanter was tricked into marrying the wrong girl (Gn 29:16–30); how he retaliated and became rich at Laban's expense (30:25–43); finally how he fled from Laban back to Canaan (Gn 31). In the account of Jacob's sons and their names, listeners could indulge their love of ingenious etymologies. (Preoccupation with names is a common Semitic characteristic. Etiologies occur about sixty times in Gn, Ex and Nm, chiefly in the Yawhist source. The Priestly writer rarely uses them and they are not even found in Lv and Dt. Some of the etiologies are entirely profane; some are cultic; others are theologized inventions which formerly had nothing to do with the salvation history.) Occasionally, it is true, there are reminders that it is Yahweh who guides and prospers the bearer of the promise (30:28; 31:7); and later portions of the cycle—the flight from Laban, the meeting with Esau and the return to Canaan—are more directly linked with Yahweh's protection of the man to whom he has tendered the promise. For the most part however the thread of salvation history is in some measure eclipsed by the profane spirit of the narrative.

Despite the blessings of prosperity and progeny Jacob is eager to return to the land promised him in the Bethel theophany. Several motives underlie his decision to go back; the most significant is Yahweh's command: "Rise now, leave this land, and return to the land of your kin" (Gn 31:13). Having obtained the consent of Rachel and Lia, Jacob sets out with his household for Canaan, once more outwitting his father-in-law. Laban's pursuit, his blustering accusations and his futile search for the household gods[14] paint a humorous picture of a clever man who has met his match. But there is more than amusement in the scene; Yahweh's protective power shines through the episode, especially when he warns Laban to do Jacob no harm

(31:24). Jacob too, in defending his conduct, pays homage to the favors of the Lord: "If the God of my father, the God of Abraham, and the God whom Isaac fears had not favored me, even now you would have sent me away empty-handed" (31:42). Wisely Laban declines to contest the divine will; he concludes a covenant with Jacob and returns home.

As Jacob advances toward Canaan he makes characteristically shrewd preparations for his encounter with Esau. Between the initial embassy (Gn 32:4–21) and the actual meeting (Gn 33) Jacob had an uncanny experience: "Someone ['*iš*] wrestled with him until dawn" (32:25). The motifs of struggle with a divinity and of a wrestling which must cease at dawn have parallels in ancient myths and demonic tales; here they have been strangely incorporated into a story of Jacob's contending with Yahweh, climaxed by a blessing and the change of his name to Israel, "because you have contended with God and men, and have triumphed" (32:30). It is difficult to harmonize all the elements of the narrative. The assailant is obviously the more powerful (he cripples Jacob by touching his thigh); yet he pleads with Jacob to release him. In his reply Jacob recognizes the superiority of his adversary: "I will not let you go till you bless me" (32:27). The divine nature of the visitation is further witnessed by the name: "Jacob named the place Phanuel, saying, 'I have seen a heavenly being ['*elohim*] face to face, yet my life has been spared'" (32:31). At best the passage is mysterious and there is little prospect of working out all its irregularities; nevertheless the essential points of blessing and change of name are clear.

In the other patriarchal narratives Yahweh's manifestations to Abraham, Isaac and Jacob were accompanied by reiterated pledges of land and posterity; such renewal of the promises is totally lacking in the story of Jacob's wrestling. The blessing and the change of the patriarch's name however are equivalent

65

to assurances of Yahweh's favor, and subsequently they are associated with the Priestly version of the promises in Gn 35:9–15 —albeit a pale reflection of the enigmatic encounter at Phanuel. When Jacob first left Canaan, Yahweh had renewed the promises and assured him of personal protection (see 28:10–22); now as Jacob returns to the land apportioned to him Yahweh again meets him and by the mysterious action at Phanuel changes the worldly-wise, crafty patriarch and raises him to new dignity— "strong against God."

Jacob's arrival in Canaan, the goal of his journey and the goal of the promise, is reported succinctly: "Jacob came safely to the city of Sichem, in the land of Chanaan. . . . For the price of one hundred pieces of money he bought the plot of ground on which he had pitched his tent, from the sons of Hemor, the father of Sichem" (Gn 33:18–19). The casual mention of Sichem betrays little hint of the prominent role this cultic center may have played in the development of the patriarchal cycles, since this sanctuary was the center of the later Israelite amphictyony.

The life of Jacob as an old man naturally did not include adventures like those of his youth. The figure of Jacob fades into the background of the Joseph story; he has little active part in Gn 37–50; but he shows traces of his old spirit in Gn 48:14–20 when he manipulates the blessings of Ephraim and Manasses. After the story of Dina (Gn 34) there are no broadly developed narratives to serve as a conclusion to the Jacob saga, only a few sparse traditions like the pilgrimage from Sichem to Bethel (Gn 35:1–8). The preparations for the pilgrimage include cultic observances more characteristic of later Yahwism than of the patriarchal religion: "Do away with the strange gods you have among you, purify yourselves, and change your garments."

Passages like the above referring to patriarchal worship raise the question: what precisely was the religion of the patriarchs?

There is no doubt that the final redaction of the Pentateuch identifies the God of Abraham, Isaac and Jacob with Yahweh, who operates throughout the whole course of Hebrew history. So much is clear. It is less certain however that the Pentateuchal picture represents the actual historical situation:

Patriarchal religion is incorporated into the integrated theological pattern of Genesis-Kings. This pattern is viewed as being rooted in history, and patriarchal religion is presented in Genesis as the historical record of Yahweh's earliest dealings with the ancestors of Israel. The dilemma confronts us: is this identification factual, or is it due to later theological rewriting of the earlier documents?[15]

The attempt to resolve the dilemma usually begins with a consideration of the divine epithets appearing in the patriarchal history: the generic term *'el* or *'elōhîm,* thought by some to be a proper name; *'el šadday,* God the Almighty, the favorite term of the Priestly writer, *'el 'elyôn,* the Most High God; *'el 'olam,* Everlasting God; and the proper name *YHWH,* Lord. The origin and meaning of these titles, as well as their relation to pre-Israelite gods, is currently the subject of extensive investigation.

The complex problem of patriarchal religion is sometimes reduced to the query: were the patriarchs polytheists or monotheists? The biblical evidence does not yield a univocal answer. According to Jos 24:2 Abraham's immediate ancestors were polytheists: "In times past your fathers down to Thare dwelt beyond the river . . . and served other gods." The household gods mentioned in Gn 31:19 show that Laban had many gods, but this fact tells nothing about the religion of Jacob. The covenant between Jacob and Laban seems to indicate Jacob's monotheism: "The God of Abraham and the gods of Nahor judge between us" (Gn 31:53). Since *'elohîm* is used for both "God" and "gods" however the passage gives no clear statement of monotheism or of polytheism. Jacob's word: "Do away with the strange gods you have among you" (Gn 35:2) again shows that those persons surrounding Jacob were polytheists, but it tells nothing about Jacob himself.

That there was growth in the revelation and knowledge of God among the Israelites is a tenet of the Priestly writer (see Ex 6:2–3). The Yahwist however assumes that Yahweh was known and worshipped from earliest times (see Gn 4:26b).

## The story of Joseph

In tone and structure the Joseph story (Gn 37–50) is a forceful contrast to the cycles which precede it. The theme of the promise so conspicuous in the lives of Abraham, Isaac and Jacob is scarcely touched on; consequently the relation of Joseph's history to salvation history is not immediately clear. Like the Jacob saga the story of Joseph displays Yahweh's subtle conversion of evil into good. Moreover the narrative as a whole documents the divine action which protects the children of the promise—Joseph and his brothers—in every vicissitude. The long biblical narrative develops without apparent divine intervention and without any advance in Yahweh's revelation; yet each stage of the composition reinforces the central theme of divine Providence epitomized in Joseph's pronouncement: "You intended evil against me, but God intended it for good, to do as he has done today, namely to save the lives of many people" (50:20; see also 45:5–8).

If the story lacks the promises which are the leitmotif of the patriarchal narratives up to this point, how does the composition advance the salvation history? By explaining how Joseph's family came to Egypt the history of Joseph bridges the gap between the themes of the patriarchal promises and the Exodus from Egypt. The saga is more than a literary synthesis however; it is salvation history, for the silent guidance of the Lord is one of his saving deeds no less than are his more vivid interventions in history. Joseph's dying words orientate the narrative to both patriarchal promises and to the Exodus: "I am about to die, but God will certainly come to you and lead you up from this land to the land which he promised on oath to Abraham, Isaac, and Jacob" (Gn 50:24; see also 46:3–4). As the cultic formula in Dt 26:5 notes, memories of a sojourn in Egypt were among the earliest traditions of Israel: "My father was a wandering Aramean who went down to Egypt with a small household and lived there as an alien." The event so briefly noted in the credo was later elaborated, perhaps within the house of Joseph, as a panegyric for a tribal ancestor. Moreover the shadow of Jacob hovers in the background as a constant reminder of the theme of the promises. Thus for example the vision at Bersabee (46:1–4) is a deliberate tie-in with the earlier theophanies at Bethel and Phanuel; the blessing the ancient patriarch pronounces on Joseph and his sons (48:15–16, 19–20) suggests the terms of the promises; and the so-called blessings of Jacob (49:1–27) anticipate the days when settlement in the promised land is a reality. These texts which link the story to salvation history are generally acknowledged to be for the most part later additions to the traditions.

## The literary structure of the Joseph saga

In addition to its contribution to the main theme of salvation history the story of Joseph commands attention on artistic grounds. Showing no interest in etiology or in separate traditions tied to persons and places, the narrative is a carefully plotted unit resembling a novella. Accurate psychological perception, both in character delineation and in motivation, gives an appeal not found in the other patriarchal stories. The brothers' hatred for Joseph (Gn 37:5–11), their deferential behavior in the

69

presence of the polished Egyptian official (42:6–17) and the gradual revelation of their change of heart (44:18ff) are credible and convincing. Moreover the judicious use of motifs enhances the unity of the work as a whole. Joseph's pretentious dreams for example motivate his brothers' hatred and prepare for the later dream interpretations which bring Joseph into favor with Pharao (Gn 40–41). Then the motif disappears, only to be evoked once again at the conclusion of the story when "his brothers came to him in person and prostrated themselves before him, saying 'We are your slaves'" (50:18).

The story of Joseph is obviously related by a non-Egyptian for non-Egyptians, but no less obvious is the fact that those who formed the traditions used Egyptian materials and techniques. The opinion long prevailed that the Egyptianisms in the narrative are a superficial coloration, dependent on shallow and confused knowledge of life in the Nile delta and that, in fact, much of what is related about Joseph is pure fiction. Recent studies have shown however that the story has roots in a deep and comprehensive knowledge of Egyptian life and may perhaps go back to Moses himself. On the other hand the literary technique and the artistry of Gn 37–50 cause the composition of these chapters to be associated with the story of Davidic succession (2 Sm 6—3 Kgs 2) in the early days of kingship.[16] The emphasis of the Davidic-Solomonic age upon humanism led in court circles to the creation of a wisdom literature geared to the education and training of young court officials. The figure of Joseph could be that of an ideal courtier exemplifying in word and act the pattern of conduct extolled in wisdom writing. The history of Joseph, like other wisdom literature, is singularly free from theological pronouncements; only at the very end does Joseph tell of the divine plan which has been operative all the while: "You intended evil against me, but God intended it for good" (Gn 50:20). This sentiment is in the best tradition of wisdom writing, which is fond of showing the contrast between human and divine modes of action:

> In his mind a man plans his course,
> But the Lord directs his steps.
>
> .  .  .  .  .  .  .  .  .  .  .
>
> Many are the plans in a man's heart,
> But it is the decision of the Lord that endures (Pv 16: 9; 19:21).

Only among a people supremely convinced that Yahweh acts in the temporal order could the patriarchal narratives grow to the proportions shown in Gn 12–50. The primitive core of the conviction is doubtless founded on the real activity of the Lord in the Exodus and at Sinai. If deliverance from Egypt and the subsequent convenant with Yahweh occurred in time and marked an advance toward divinely appointed ends, then the period before these events must likewise be orientated to future goals. Hence the era before the Exodus and Sinai is not sheer empty time but a period of initial revelation of divine goals, a time of gradual progress toward their attainment. Progeny and land were the two great promises given in the first disclosure of Yahweh's plan. In the patriarchal history the traditions dwell principally on the first of these promises, i.e. how the childless Abraham, despite obstacles of every kind, secured a numerous posterity flourishing in the land of Egypt. The fullfillment of the first promise is itself a pledge that Yahweh will be no less faithful in accomplishing the second; but its attainment must be in Yahweh's time and in his own way.

## Themes of the Exodus

The narrative of the divine action in favor of the patriarchs constitutes a prelude to the tradition which Israel perpetually maintained as the most glorious example of Yahweh's work

71

in her behalf: deliverance from Egypt and guidance to the promised land. The tremendous impact of the Exodus tradition on the religion and history of Israel is undeniable; it is the first of Yahweh's mighty deeds, the cell from which all Israelite theology developed. To this work of the Lord Israel attributed her whole existence and her exceptional place in the circle of nations. Memories of rescue from "that iron foundry, Egypt" (Dt 4:20) recur constantly within the traditions of the Pentateuch and beyond it. Wherever Yahweh's powerful acts are recalled, whether in the narratives or in the legislative sections, there the Exodus is brought first to mind, frequently by the hymnic epithet "Yahweh, your God, who brought you out of the land of Egypt," as in Ex 20:2. The narratives in the Deuteronomic histories usually recall deliverance from Egypt as a sign of Yahweh's continued help in the present and future: "For we have heard how the Lord dried up the waters of the Red Sea before you when you came out of Egypt" (Jos 2:10). Sometimes they invoke the Exodus as a motive for gratitude and obedience, as in 1 Sm 10:18. In the prophetic admonitions it is Yahweh himself who reminds the people how they were rescued: "I brought you up from the land of Egypt, from the place of slavery I released you" (Mi 6:4); and "When Israel was a child I loved him, out of Egypt I called my son" (Os 11:1). In the psalms the escape from Egypt is frequently proposed as a motive for praise (see Pss 78:12ff; 135:8–9). The motif of miraculous delivery from slavery continues to exert its influence in Christian times; it figures prominently in the typology of the Fathers and in the prayer life of the Church. A favorite theme of patristic typology is the correlation of events of the Exodus with the rites of Christian initiation.

Israelite cult evoked the Exodus theme by deliberately aligning the primitive Passover feast with deliverance from Egypt. Three times Dt gives this orientation:

Observe the month of Abib by keeping the Passover of the Lord, your God, since it was in the month of Abib that he brought you by night out of Egypt. . . . For seven days you shall eat with it only unleavened bread, the bread of affliction, that you may remember as long as you live the day of your departure from the land of Egypt; for in frightened haste you left the land of Egypt. . . . In the evening at sunset, on the anniversary of your departure from Egypt, you shall sacrifice the Passover (16:1, 3, 6).

Exodus and Passover are similarly associated in the festal legislation of Ex 12:23 and 34:18. (Lv 23:43 however links the Exodus with the Feast of Tabernacles.) The parenesis woven into the social legislation also recalls the hard days in Egypt as a motive for kindly treatment of slaves and resident strangers: "For remember that you too were once slaves in the land of Egypt, and the Lord, your God, ransomed you" (Dt 15:15); and "So you too must befriend the alien, for you were once aliens yourselves in the land of Egypt" (10:19).

Among the earliest texts commemorating deliverance from Egypt are the so-called cultic credos of Dt 6 and 26, both of which associate the Exodus with the tradition of acquisition of the land:

We were once slaves of Pharao in Egypt, but the Lord brought us out of Egypt with his strong hand and wrought before our eyes signs and wonders, great and dire, against Egypt and against Pharao and his whole house. He brought us from there to lead us into the land he promised on oath to our fathers, and to give it to us (6: 21–23).

My father was a wandering Aramean who went down to Egypt with a small household and lived there as an alien. But there he became a nation great, strong and numerous. When the Egyptians maltreated and oppressed us, imposing hard labor upon us, we cried to the Lord, the God of our fathers, and he heard our cry and saw our affliction, our toil and our oppression. He brought us out of Egypt with his strong hand and outstretched arm, with terrifying power, with signs and wonders; and bringing us into this country, he gave us this land flowing with milk and honey (26: 5–9).

Although Deuteronomic phraseology permeates the two passages the rhythmic and alliterative pattern indicates their great age. If the credos circulated orally for a long period of time before being written down (and this seems to be the case), their use would assume a rendition of salvation history which became quasi-canonical at a very early age. The stylized structure of the cultic confessions does not permit elaboration of the Exodus events, but the salient features of Egyptian oppression and divine rescue appear even in these abbreviated accounts.

## Themes of oppression and deliverance

The basic facts mentioned succinctly in the cultic credos are rounded out in Ex 1–15, where separate traditions have been combined to display many aspects of Yahweh's activity in favor of Israel. So strong is the conviction that the Lord had marvelously rescued his people, so forcefully does the theme of deliverance pervade the Old Testament writings that it is necessary to posit an extraordinary historical event occasioning the conviction. The event itself however remains veiled. The persons involved, the date, the circumstances—these are matters which cannot at present be accurately determined. 3 Kgs 6:1 places the Exodus four hundred and eighty years before the fourth year of Solomon's reign, i.e. about 1438. There are reasons to question this date: the artificiality of the chronology (twelve generations reckoned at forty years each) and the archeological evidence unfavorable to so early a date.

The consensus of modern critics is that the Pharao of the oppression was Seti I (1302–1290) and that the long-lived Rameses II (1290–1224) was the Pharao of the Exodus. Some scholars however identify Rameses II as the Pharao of the oppression and his successor, Merneptah (1224–1214), as the Pharao of the Exodus. Although critics generally agree that the

74

oppression and the Exodus fall within the nineteenth dynasty, probably between 1302 and 1214, others hold that a double exodus occurred, the first about 1400 and the second about 1250. In any event the tradition of deliverance became the property of all Israel, but this does not mean that all the tribes took part in the historical Exodus. One can only say that the people of the Exodus were elements from which the tribes of united Israel were subsequently formed.

The cultic credos refer briefly to the hard lot of the Hebrews in Egypt: "We were once slaves of Pharao in Egypt" (Dt 6:21); and "the Egyptians maltreated and oppressed us, imposing hard labor upon us" (26:6). With greater detail Ex 1 elaborates the theme of persecution by a description of successively more oppressive measures which the Pharao "who knew nothing of Joseph" employed against the Hebrews: forced labor, enslavement, inhuman killing of newborn males. In the enumeration of miseries separate traditions have been combined into larger units without our modern attention to proportion and emphasis; the story of the death of the newborn Hebrew males for instance has retained the names of the midwives, Sephra and Phua, but does not identify the Pharao (Ex 1:15).

Harried and bereft, the Israelites had no happy prospects either for themselves or for their posterity. At this point Moses appears. Although he dominates four books of the Pentateuch there is little that can be said about him with certainty. All traditions are unanimous however in according him the pre-eminent role as organizer of his people, as legislator and as the founder of Yahwism.[17] Born during the oppression, Moses was providentially saved and reared, according to a non-Pentateuchal tradition, "in all the wisdom of the Egyptians" (Acts 7:22). Forced to flee Egypt (Ex 2:11–16) he took refuge in Madian in southern Arabia, south of Edom and east of the Gulf of Aqaba. Moses' relation to the Madianites (or more precisely to one of their tribes, the Kenites; see Jgs 4:11) has assumed new importance upon the adoption by some scholars of the Kenite theory of Yahwism. Since it was in Madian that Yahweh first appeared to Moses it has been suggested that Yahweh was the local god of the Kenites and that Moses adopted the worship of the place. Proponents of the hypothesis find additional support in Ex 18; Moses' father-in-law, the Kenite priest Jethro, offers sacrifice in Moses' presence and states: "Blessed be the Lord . . . who has rescued his people from the hands of Pharao and the Egyptians. Now I know that the Lord is a deity great beyond any other" (18:10–11).

In Madian Yahweh revealed himself and laid upon Moses the task of leading the Israelites out of Egypt. The portentous commission, so pregnant with vital consequences for all Hebrew history, is enhanced by the episode of the burning bush. From the midst of the fire Yahweh identified himself as "the God of your father, . . . the God of Abraham, the God of Isaac, the God of Jacob" (Ex 3:6). This Kenite theory of Yahwism (a favorite thesis with H. H. Rowley) has not found general acceptance.

As always in the salvation history Yahweh takes the initiative and commissions Moses to deliver the Hebrews. And, as always, human weakness is unable to take Yahweh at his word. Moses protests: "Who am I . . . ?" (Ex 3:11); "But suppose . . ." (4:1); "If you please, . . ." (4:13). But the divine will brooks no opposition. A second tradition of Moses' appointment is preserved in the Priestly writing of 6:2—7:13. The repetition of substantially the same account indicates the great significance Israel attached to this event (especially as regards the revelation of the divine name), but the retention of the second narrative is occasioned by another reason. By inserting the events of 6:2 —7:13 after the similar JE narrative of 3:1ff and after the story of Moses' first encounter with Pharao (5:1ff), the redactor has presented the Priestly version of Moses' appointment as a

76

confirmation of the original commission and as a summons to continued negotiations with Pharao.

The commission of Moses also gives the Priestly writer the opportunity to recount the revelation of the name "Yahweh." According to Yahwist traditions this divine name was known almost from the beginning; the conclusion of the Kenite genealogy reads: "At that time men began to call upon the name of the Lord" (Gn 4: 26b; see also 13:4, where Abraham calls upon the name of the Lord). It is in keeping with the universalist theology of the Yahwist that he should trace the worship of Yahweh to the origins of the world. The Elohist tradition on the other hand indicates that the name was not known until Moses' question brought its disclosure (Ex 3:13–14). What the Elohist implies the Priestly author makes explicit: "God also said to Moses, 'I am the Lord. As God the Almighty I appeared to Abraham, Isaac, and Jacob, but my name, Lord, I did not make known to them' " (Ex 6:2–3). The Priestly writer is here emphasizing the special character of Hebrew religion by linking revelation of the divine name with the events which led to the constitution of Yahwism.

The etymology of the word "Yahweh" has not been resolved to universal satisfaction; even if it could be, the etymology arrived at by modern philology would not necessarily be that of the sacred writer. A widely accepted view is that the name is a third-person form from the root *HYH* (earlier *HWY* and *HWH*) meaning to fall, to become or to come into existence; thus the form *yahweh* means "he causes to be what comes into existence." Originally the name may have had a longer litanic phrasing, such as *Yahweh sābaʿôt*—"he who creates the hosts of Israel."

Yahweh revealed to Moses his name: "*Ehyeh ʾašer ʾehyeh*" —"I am who I am." Then he said: "This is what you shall tell the Israelites: 'I AM sent me to you' " (Ex 3:14). This translation has led to the interpretation common among Catholic philosophers and theologians that the proper name of God is Being. It is highly improbable however that the Semitic writer entertained such abstractions as being-as-such or asseity. The interpretation is based moreover on the Septuagint's mistranslation of the Hebrew form, which was doubtless a causative.

Some critics contend that Yahweh's answer is equivalent to a refusal to tell his name.[18] Among the ancients knowledge of a person's name was supposed to give power over the person. Moses' question then is not prompted by ignorance of the divine title but by a desire to know its essential meaning. Yahweh's answer indicates that God is not to be comprehended by the creature. Such a reading is justified by adducing biblical parallels in which the reduplication of the verb shows nuances of indetermination as in 1 Sm 23:13. Yahweh answers Moses: "I am who I am," i.e. "I will not tell you who I am."

But the meaning of the divine name cannot be based on etymology and syntax alone. The context must also be considered, and the context suggests that God is really telling his name, not refusing to disclose it. Since the Priestly writer is very insistent that the divine name was revealed only at the time of Moses the true meaning of the name seems peculiarly associated with the events of the Exodus, and perhaps with the Sinai covenant which followed. Even the Yahwist, who assumes the name was known from earliest times, links to the Sinai covenant a special proclamation of God's name: "He [Yahweh] answered, 'I will make all my beauty pass before you, and in your presence I will pronounce my name, "Lord;" I who show favors to whom I will, I who grant mercy to whom I will'" (Ex 33:19); and again: "Having come down in a cloud, the Lord stood with him there, and proclaimed his name, 'Lord'" (34:5). In the final analysis however it seems impossible at present to determine the exact significance of the divine name for the Mosaic age. Given the context of Exodus and Sinai, the name refers to God as dynamically present to his people for the accomplishment of their salvation.

## The contest with Pharao

The pace of the narrative accelerates as it depicts the struggle between Yahweh and Pharao, who repeatedly refuses permission for a festal celebration in the desert and imposes still heavier burdens upon the Hebrews (Ex 5:6–13). The royal obduracy is answered by the wondrous signs Yahweh had promised in chs 3, 4 and 7. The plague stories are secondary traditions developed and unified to translate into concrete terms Israel's realization of Yahweh as her champion against the forces that would enslave and crush her. The stories of the plagues in Ex 7:14—11:10 are mainly from the Yahwist and Priestly traditions, with occasional additions from the Elohist. The Priestly tradition emphasizes, as might be expected, the part of Aaron in the performance of the wonders; with his staff he produces the first three plagues and in each case confounds the magicians. The staff of Moses is also important (see 4:1–5, 17:15–17; 9:23; 10:13). The Elohist, though, stresses the hand of Moses in the accomplishment of the marvels (see 9:22; 10:12, 21; 14:21).

Each encounter between Moses and Pharao brings to nought the occult devices of the royal magicians, until finally the latter admit "the finger of God," thus vindicating the power at work in Moses and Aaron (8:14–15). The suspense of the narrative mounts as the king himself shows signs of weakening. The Israelites may leave if they pray for him (8:24); only the men may leave (10:11); the children may leave but the flocks and herds must remain (10:24). In a sense however each of the plague stories ends in an impasse; despite successive, undeniable manifestations of Yahweh's supreme mastery Pharao obstinately

79

refuses to let the Hebrews depart—and then the whole situation is repeated in the account of the next plague. The motif of Pharao's obstinacy, referred to more than a dozen times in the plague narratives, further exemplifies Yahweh's sovereign control: "But the Lord made Pharao obstinate, and he would not listen to them" (9:12; see also 7:3; 10:1; 11:10). A creature's obduracy cannot shatter the divine plans, for Pharao no less than Moses is an instrument of Yahweh, and the power of the Lord is only magnified by all that men can do to thwart it.

The unified plague stories were put at the service of the Passover narrative, which is their climax; and the entire complex—plagues and Passover—was consciously employed to illustrate the salvific power which found supreme expression in the Exodus. It appears that the plagues are natural phenomena to be expected in Egypt; yet the disasters are certainly not described as natural phenomena but as prodigious deeds of Yahweh working through his servants Moses and Aaron. The stories may be rooted in folklore, but in a folklore utilized to extol Yahweh's free disposition of man and natural forces, to answer Pharao's insolent query: "Who is the Lord, that I should heed his plea to let Israel go?" (Ex 5:2).

Modern philosophy of nature does not recognize the divine action in ordinary physical events. Plagues, whether they are called natural phenomena or even extraordinary natural phenomena, do not belong in the realm of the marvelous. Among the Hebrews however the consciousness of Yahweh's activity in the universe was so keen that even natural phenomena were esteemed wonderful and mysterious: every work of the Lord is marvelous. This Hebrew concept is admirably shown in the happenings of the Exodus; what is remarkable about the plagues is not so much the phenomena themselves as the fact that Yahweh used these events to accomplish the rescue of his people. And although the modern critic must try to ascertain what natural forces were at work in the biblical stories of the plagues, the attempt to reduce the afflictions to a series of specific, integrated events has not as yet been successful.

As the affliction touching the Egyptians most cruelly the death of the firstborn properly climaxes the series of punishments sent against Pharao and his people. The life setting and attendant circumstances are unknown; the terse account of the fulfilled threat simply reports: "At midnight the Lord slew every firstborn in the land of Egypt, from the firstborn of Pharao on the throne to the firstborn of the prisoner in the dungeon, as well as the firstborn of the animals" (Ex 12:29). The killing of the firstborn impressed itself deeply upon Hebrew thought: first, because of its natural significance as the climax of the plagues; second, because of its association with the Feast of Passover, the meaning of which was greatly modified by the new orientation.

According to Ex 12-21 the Passover was probably a feast celebrated by the Hebrews while they were still in Egypt, although its precise significance is not known. The feast may have been one kept by nomads before moving to new grounds. In this case it would logically be associated by the Hebrews with their final break with Egypt, and the Passover sacrifice would be directed against the evil powers represented by Egypt. The account of these evils might naturally include the plagues. The Priestly writer links the old nomadic shepherd feast with the escape from Egypt and decrees its celebration as a perpetual ordinance: "When your children ask you: 'What does this rite of yours mean?' you shall reply, 'This is the Passover sacrifice of the Lord, who passed over the house of the Israelites in Egypt; when he struck down the Egyptians, he spared our houses'" (Ex 12:27). The ritual directions likewise connect the Passover with the Feast of Unleavened Bread, perhaps originally a separate celebration. The sacred writer attributes the origin of

81

this feast to the commemoration of the hasty departure from Egypt when the Hebrews carried only unleavened bread with them (see 12:34, 39).

## The Exodus proper

The event of the Exodus itself is difficult to follow not only because details are lacking but also because conflicting traditions have been retained. The manner of the Hebrews' departure is reported in different ways. The principal tradition affirms that Pharao granted permission to leave after the death of his firstborn son, but traces of another tradition suggest that the departure was unknown to him: "When it was reported to the king of Egypt that the people had fled, Pharao and his servants changed their minds about them" (Ex 14:5). The story of the despoliation of the Egyptians (3:21–22; 11:2–3; 12:33–36) is not easily reconciled with the main tradition. That the Egyptians should urge the Hebrews to leave is understandable; that they should be well disposed and grant them silver, gold and clothing is less readily comprehensible. In addition the chronological relationship between the events is very obscure. The Passover ritual following the threat of the tenth plague implies that the three happenings—death of the firstborn, Passover and escape from Egypt—transpired in a single night (see 12:11, 31, 50–51); but variant traditions have been kept. In Ex 12:21–23 the Hebrews are told not to depart until morning; according to 12:30ff their flight evidently took place during the night. The Passover directions (12:1ff) indicate that the people are prepared for the flight which follows but other passages show that their departure was unexpected (see 12:33–36, 39).

What route the Israelites followed when they made good their escape is likewise not certain. Rameses, a city in the eastern part of the Nile delta, is named as their point of departure (Ex 12:37), and the tradition specifies that the people were not led "by way of the Philistines' land," i.e. directly along the shores of the Mediterranean, but rather "toward the Red Sea by way of the desert road" (13:17, 18). Despite these and other indications (Nm 33) their exact itinerary is not known, although new identifications of place names are continually being made. Finally there is no way of ascertaining the number of Israelites taking part in the Exodus. Ex 12:37 says 600,000 men but this total is far too high. A group of this size would imply a total population of nearly three million. The departure of such a horde—plus flocks and herds—is an utter impossibility. Moreover the country through which they marched could not conceivably sustain them. It is useless to conjecture what the original figure may have been.

The stirring display of Yahweh's protection during the plagues leads up to the supreme feat of the Exodus: the passage of the Hebrews through the Red Sea, more correctly translated as Reed Sea (*yâm sûf*). Very probably it is the Papyrus Sea or Marsh Sea located in the northeastern Nile delta, a southern extension of the present Menzahleh Lake in the Mediterranean. The entire region is near the modern Suez Canal. Here again the actual event is obscure because two variant traditions have been preserved. One tradition relates how Moses is told to take his staff and with outstretched hand to split the sea in two (Ex 14:16); another recounts how the Lord swept the sea with a strong east wind and transformed it into dry land (14:21). The fate of the Egyptians is variously described. Yahweh with a glance throws their forces into panic and clogs the chariot wheels so that they could not easily drive (14:24–25). In a variant tradition Yahweh commands Moses: "Stretch our your hand over the sea, that the water may flow back upon the Egyptians, upon their chariots, and their charioteers" (14:26). And in v 27 it is related that "the Egyptians were fleeing head

83

on toward the sea, when the Lord hurled them into its midst." The divine protection is also described in parallel traditions. The Elohist version tells that the angel of Yahweh, who had been leading the camp of Israel, moved to the rear (14:19a). In the Yahwist tradition the divine presence is represented by a column of cloud coming between the Egyptians and the Israelites (14:19b–20). These discrepancies do not touch the main issue since the historical facts of the situation are not of supreme moment. What matters—and this could not be uttered with greater clarity—is that "the Lord saved Israel on that day from the power of the Egyptians" (14:30), a fact which Israel recognized in Miriam's chant: "Sing to the Lord, for he is gloriously triumphant; horse and chariot he has cast into the sea" (15:21b).

## The wandering in the desert

The theme of desert wandering connects the motifs of the Exodus with those of the conquest of the promised land. At one time the stories composing the history of the desert sojourn were undoubtedly independent narratives with a life setting now beyond recovery. In some cases the stories are quite old, although they assumed their position in the sacred traditions only at a later date. The wonder wrought at the Red Sea was a striking augury of Yahweh's solicitude for his people all the days of their wandering, days when he carried Israel "as a man carries his child" (Dt 1:31). He furnished them water (Ex 15:22ff; 17:1ff); he sent manna for their food (16:4–36; Nm 11:6–9); and he condescended to their desire for meat by giving them quail (Ex 16:12–13; Nm 11:31–34). Dt gives equally impressive evidence of the divine protection: "The clothing did not fall from you in tatters, nor did your feet swell these forty years" (Dt 8:4; see also 29:5). During the early days in the desert Yahweh helped the Israelites defeat the Amalecites, Bedouin marauders of Sinai and southern Palestine (Ex 17:8–16), and throughout their wanderings he continued to support them in battle (Ex 21). Not content with satisfying their physical needs and with defeating their foes Yahweh preceded the Israelites in a pillar of cloud by day and a column of fire by night (Ex 13:21–22; Dt 1:33). A variant tradition recalls how the angel of the Lord was sent as a guide (Ex 14:19; Nm 20:16).

And what was the response of the Hebrews? The absorbing recital of the plagues and the negotiations between Moses and Pharao left scant opportunity for noting the reaction of the Hebrews. At the start of Moses' mission it was stated: "The people believed, and when they had heard that the Lord was concerned about them and had seen their affliction, they bowed down in worship" (Ex 4:31). Even in Egypt however some among them opposed Moses, for when they saw the Egyptians in pursuit they bitterly reminded him: "Why did you bring us out of Egypt? Did we not tell you this in Egypt when we said, 'Leave us alone. Let us serve the Egyptians'" (14:11–12). Later, awed by the exercise of divine power against Egypt at the Red Sea, "they feared the Lord and believed in him and in his servant Moses" (14:31). But scarcely were they out of Egypt when they began that steady stream of complaints which brand their years in the desert both before and after Sinai. Salvation history records not only Yahweh's deeds but also the interplay of human and divine activity—Yahweh's offer of grace and man's response. The murmurings in the desert document Israel's ungrateful response to all that Yahweh had effected in her behalf. Perhaps the stories are not a part of the original traditions of salvation history. But the narratives of the murmurings are so deeply imbedded in the traditions that they may be regarded as a very early theological concept of the mystery of proffered salvation and its rejection.

Thus after only three days' journey from the Red Sea the

Hebrews grumbled because of the bitter waters of Mara (Ex 15:22–25). Again at Raphidim they quarreled with Moses: "Why did you ever make us leave Egypt? Was it just to have us die here of thirst with our children and our livestock?" (17:3; see also Nm 20:4). In both cases Yahweh listens to Moses' appeal and grants water to the maundering Israelites. The contrast between human petulance and divine condescension, between man's selfishness and Yahweh's generosity effectively reveals the utter gratuity of salvation. Doubtless these stories were at one time popular etiologies of the place name Mara (bitter), Massa (testing) and Meriba (quarrel); one need not think that the narratives pretend to catalogue actual day-to-day events of the desert sojourn. Rather they have been amalgamated with the other traditions in order to point up the relation between Yahweh and his people more vividly and completely. Another etiological tale provides the foundation of Nm 11:1–3. When the people complained, "the fire of the Lord burned among them and consumed the outskirts of the camp. . . . Hence that place was called Thabera, because there the fire of the Lord burned among them."

Once more, longing for the hearty fare of Egypt, the Hebrews received the Lord's promise: "I will now rain down bread from heaven for you" (Ex 16:4). The story of the manna has been elaborated beyond the theme of murmuring but there is little doubt that its original core belongs to the narratives of the Israelite complaints. The meticulous directions concerning the manna, e.g. Moses' instructions to place an urn of manna in front of the Commandments (Ex 16:32–34), are a result of later reworking. The Deuteronomist sees a new lesson in the manna: "He therefore let you be afflicted with hunger, and then fed you with manna, a food unknown to you and your fathers, in order to show you that not by bread alone does man live, but by every word that comes forth from the mouth of the

Lord" (Dt 8:3). Ex 16 mentions briefly the quail sent by the Lord (vv 8, 12, 13); a more forceful story in Nm 11 tells that this meat-food was given them after the complaint: "Would that we had meat for food" (Nm 11:18). Their greed brought swift punishment: "While the meat was still between their teeth, before it could be consumed, the Lord's wrath flared up against the people, and he struck them with a very great plague. So that place was named Cibroth-Hatthaava, because it was there that the greedy people were buried" (Nm 11:33–34).

Later these rebellious murmurings brought equally strict sanctions from Yahweh. After the death of Aaron the complaints of the Israelites were punished by the stings of saraph serpents. (The serpent pericope seems a latecomer to the traditions of desert murmuring. As 4 Kgs 18:4 indicates, its point of origin was very likely the bronze serpent idol which until the time of Hesekia was honored as a cultic symbol dating from the time of Moses. The story may have arisen to legitimatize the popular cult.) Only when the Israelites acknowledged their guilt and begged Moses' intercession did the Lord remove the affliction. Again, struck with fear at the scouts' report of a land defended by fierce inhabitants in fortified towns, the people reviled Moses, who nonetheless interceded for them (Nm 14:1–38; Dt 1:26–40). The Lord answered:

I pardon them as you have asked. Yet, by my life and the Lord's glory that fills the whole earth, of all the men who have seen my glory and the signs I have worked in Egypt and in the desert, and who nevertheless have put me to the test ten times already and have failed to heed my voice, not one shall see the land which I promised on oath to their fathers (Nm 14: 20–22).

Most frequently the murmurings are directed against Moses (or Moses and Aaron) as Yahweh's representative, and usually there is nothing personal in the Israelites' charges. In two stories however the complaints are obviously dictated by personal re-

87

sentment. The murmurings of Miriam and Aaron (Nm 12:1–15) are based on rancor over Moses' marriage to a Chusite woman and on jealousy of the favors Moses had received from Yahweh.

Later Core, Dathan and Abiram rebel against Moses' domination (Nm 16 and 17). The pericopes include two distinct rebellions: the religious uprising of Core (Nm 16:1–11, 16–24; Nm 17) and the revolt of the Rubenites Dathan and Abiram (Nm 16:13–15, 25–34; Dt 11:6). A desire to extol the Aaronite priesthood was probably one reason for the development of the Core narrative.

Even the conduct of Moses was not free from reproach. At Cades when they struck the rock to secure water for the Hebrews, Moses and Aaron incurred Yahweh's displeasure because they failed to manifest his sanctity to Israel (Nm 20:2ff). As a punishment they were not allowed to enter the land of promise. Ultimately it remains mysterious why the performance of the brothers on this occasion should prompt Yahweh to forbid them entry into Palestine.

Grumbling and murmuring led the Israelites to overt rebellion against the Lord in the worship of the golden calf (Ex 32) and in the sacrifices made to Baal Phogor (Nm 25). The ingratitude and stubborn resistance which characterized their response to divine favors earned for them Yahweh's epithet "stiff-necked people" (Ex 32:9; Dt 9:13). Although the memory of rebellious Israel in the desert is not lost for later writers (see Os 9:10; 11:1–2), it is interesting to note how this period is idealized in the prophetic books. Jeremia recalls: "I remember the devotion of your youth, how you loved me as a bride, following me in the desert in a land unsown" (2:2); and Osee looks for a return of that blissful time: "So I will allure her; I will lead her into the desert and speak to her heart. . . . She shall respond there as in the days of her youth, when she came up from the land of

Egypt" (2:16–17b). Israel by the time of the prophets had repeatedly spurned the divine overtures and had accumulated a sorry record of failures. Yahweh's lasting covenant guaranteed opportunity for a fresh start and a zealous response in each and every age; yet the prophets thought nostalgically of the pristine desert milieu as the ideal circumstance for worthy response to the invitation of the Lord.

## The Sinai theme

Conscious of election by Yahweh, Israel recognized herself as his special possession, dearer to him than all other peoples of the earth. That election—present germinally in the promises to the patriarchs and singularly indicated by the Exodus with its subsequent protection in the desert—Yahweh ratified at Sinai by a covenant not with a single individual (as he had made with Noe and Abraham), but with all Israel. By the terms of the alliance Yahweh became in a special manner the God of the Israelites and they became his people. In the persons of her ancestors Israel for many generations had realized Yahweh's predilection and had responded to it; never before Sinai however were the full implications of both election and response brought home to her so forcibly. Like the Exodus materials the Sinai tradition has its roots in history, but the Pentateuchal records yield no meticulous reports of events in orderly sequence. Although it is impossible to correlate the variant traditions satisfactorily the central message is strong and clear: at Sinai Yahweh revealed himself to Israel, inaugurated a unique covenantal relationship with his people and, by disclosing his moral will, provided the means to guarantee continued life within the covenant's bonds. Since the covenantal nature of the relationship between Yahweh and Israel will be discussed later it will here suffice to examine the Sinai theophany in general and to show its role in the formation of Israel's concept of salvation history.

The tradition of divine revelation at Sinai is vital to Yahwism. Not community of blood, or of land or of government but alliance with the Lord united the "crowd of mixed ancestry" (Ex 12:38) which fled Egypt. The course of early Israelite history, in which the sense of religious solidarity is bound up with the Sinai tradition, shows that the covenantal union established on the mountain of God is an original element in all sources, and it testifies to the factual character of the divine revelation. The evidence of later Yahwism also witnesses the primacy of the covenantal theme: the prophets reproach Israel for her great sin—betrayal of her election, rejection of the gifts and leadership of Yahweh. Surprisingly enough however the Sinai tradition long maintained its independence of other Pentateuchal traditions. The ancient cultic credos of Dt 6 and 26 pass immediately from the Exodus to entrance into the promised land, with no mention of the divine encounter at Sinai. The omission is the more striking because Dt 6:21ff purports to explain the meaning of the ordinances, statutes and decrees enjoined by the Lord—legislation bestowed at the time the covenant was initiated. Outside the Pentateuch the association of Sinai with other elements of salvation history became popular only in postexilic days; Ps 106 and the prayer of Nehemia (Neh 9:6ff) contain the first instances of the Sinai material joined to the other traditions of salvation history.

The dearth of references to the covenant in early texts and the relatively late association of the Sinai material to companion themes have occasioned the opinion that the Sinai tradition arose much later than the primitive traditions of the Exodus and the conquest of the promised land. Following Wellhausen many critics viewed the Sinai pericope as an interruption of the events at Cades, the account of which is broken off at the end of Ex 18 and resumed in Nm 10–14. Whatever Israel received in the way of law, according to Wellhausen, she received at Mara: "It was here that the Lord, in making rules and regulations for them, put them to the test" (Ex 15:25b). Therefore the critics regarded the ancient significance of Sinai as independent of any covenant or imposition of law. The late incorporation of so important a concept as the Sinai covenant into the Pentateuchal traditions does pose a problem, but to argue that because the Sinai tradition is absent from the earliest texts it therefore did not exist is to reconstruct the history and religion of Israel by literary criticism exclusively. After all, the only legitimate and safe starting point for an examination of Israel's relation to Yahweh is the evidence of the Old Testament taken as a whole: the worship of Yahweh was based on the covenantal agreement the Lord himself had established for Israel at Sinai. And the force and influence of the Sinai tradition are such that the theme must be accounted an independent primitive tradition in Israel.

Why the traditions of the covenant circulated independently and were not united with other themes in the preliterary stages of the Pentateuch is difficult to ascertain.[19] Perhaps it was because the revelation at Sinai was unique among Yahweh's saving acts. Israel's experience at Sinai differed from all her previous experiences of Yahweh because it was an encounter binding her to his declared moral will. To a degree therefore it is understandable why the events of Sinai would not readily be combined with other recollections of Yahweh's mighty deeds; the very uniqueness of the revelation kept it a thing apart. Sinai is primarily an encounter with Yahweh; therefore its traditions are kept separate from the cultic commemoration of Yahweh's salvific acts.

## The Pentateuchal traditions of Sinai

The experiences of Israel at Sinai are recorded in Ex 19–24 (with supplementary matter in Ex 32–34) and, more briefly, in Dt 4:9–15; 5:1–5. Of the accounts in Ex almost four chapters are devoted to law (the Decalogue, Ex 20:2–17; and the Code of the Covenant, Ex 20:22—23: 19), leaving a scant sixty verses to report the divine meeting so crucial to Yahwism. Because different traditions have been juxtaposed in these verses it is almost impossible to determine the sequence of events. Critics hold that both the Yahwist and the Elohist are represented in the Sinai narrative but there is little agreement on the sections to be assigned to each. Moreover some portions of the narrative, such as Ex 19:3–9 and 23:20–33, are almost certainly later additions. While the Israelites camped in the desert near the mountain of God[20] Yahweh bade Moses prepare the people for a theophany on the third day; all were to sanctify themselves and carefully avoid the sacred mountain as forbidden territory (see Ex 19:12–13). Then "on the morning of the third day there were peals of thunder and lightning, and a heavy cloud over the mountain, and a very loud trumpet blast. . . . The smoke rose from it as though from a furnace, and the whole mountain trembled violently" (Ex 19:16, 18b). Dt further states that the mountain was ablaze with fire (4:11; 5:23–26).

The phenomena accompanying the theophany are those of a storm and a violent volcanic eruption. The unusual combination has caused some critics to seek earnestly for geographic and climatic conditions which will account for the phenomena in their least details; they forget that the essential note of the theophany is the divine activity manifested in physical phenomena, which the sacred writer may have constructed so as best to convey the principal idea. Because a storm was linked with the event through which Israel was initiated into the covenant so vital to her religion, the storm theophany became the chief model for the depiction of subsequent divine manifestations—e.g. in the psalms.

The traditions vary in reporting what, if anything, the people saw in addition to the signs and wonders accompanying Yahweh's revelation. Ex 19:11 notes: "On the third day the Lord will come down on Mount Sinai before the eyes of all the people" (see also Ex 19:17); and Dt 5:4 recalls: "The Lord spoke to you face to face on the mountain from the midst of the fire." But in other passages the Hebrews only hear the words addressed by Yahweh to Moses or to themselves: "Then the Lord spoke to you from the midst of the fire. You heard the sound of the words, but saw no form; there was only a voice" (Dt 4:12; also Ex 19:19). Throughout the narrative Moses mediates between Yahweh and the people. Moses alone is permitted to approach God upon the holy mountain (see Ex 19:12ff; 24:2). Through him Yahweh gave directions to the people: "Thus shall you speak to the Israelites. . . ." (Ex 20:22); and through Moses the people respond to Yahweh: "We will do everything that the Lord has told us" (Ex 24:3).

The awesome phenomena occurring on Mount Sinai are but accouterments to the essence of the theophany: the revelation of Yahweh's will to establish a personal alliance with Israel. Unfortunately the texts provide scanty information on the exact nature of the covenant revealed by Yahweh. The stress upon law in Ex 19–24 by reason of the insertion of the Decalogue and the Code of the Covenant into the Sinai context suggests that the chief element in the Sinai encounter is the disclosure of divine moral law for Israel. At times the covenant (*berît*) is even equated with law: "And he wrote on the tablets the words of the covenant, the Ten Commandments" (Ex 34:28; see also Dt 4:13). Elsewhere however there are indications that the covenantal agreement is distinct from the commands which accompany it: "This is the blood of the covenant which the Lord has made with you in accordance with all these words of his" (Ex 24:8; see also 34:27).

The traditions of covenant ratification appear in Ex 24:2–11. According to one tradition—vv 1–2, 9–11—Moses and the seventy elders ascended the holy mountain and there, after seeing the God of Israel, partook of a sacred meal. Although ratification is not mentioned in the verses it could be that the sacred banquet, by symbolizing community of life and interests among the participants, was regarded as a seal of the relationship established. There is no question of Yahweh participating in the meal. But the banquet in his presence is nevertheless a symbol of the communion established with Yahweh through the covenant. The second tradition (vv 3–8) tells of solemn sacrifices at the foot of Mount Sinai in confirmation of the people's promise to heed all that the Lord had told them. In this pericope the ceremony of ratification is quite clear. After sprinkling blood upon the altar Moses read the Israelites the Book of the Covenant. Then he sprinkled blood upon the people, saying: "This is the blood of the covenant which the Lord has made with you in accordance with all these words of his" (Ex 24:8). Christ's explicit reference to these ceremonies at Sinai shows the continuing centrality of the covenant in Christianity. On the eve of his passion, which was to inaugurate a new dispensation, Jesus instituted the sacrament of his body and blood with the words: "This is my blood of the new covenant, which is being shed for many" (Mk 14:24).

The Sinai block proper (Ex 19–24) is supplemented by chs 32–34, which contain additional pericopes loosely related to the core of Yahweh's revelation on Sinai. Israel's worship of the golden calf is the center of interest in these chapters. More than once did Israel turn from Yahweh and spurn his covenant. In the episode of the golden calf the sacred writer has recapitulated this continual series of rejections. A supplement to the Sinai tradition, the story of the golden calf is doubtless a polemic against the calf worship introduced by Jeroboam I in Dan and Bethel (3 Kgs 12:28b). Discrepancies and a certain unevenness indicate that the tradition suffered many accretions. From the proclamation: "Tomorrow is a feast of the Lord" it would appear that the calf was not intended as an idol but as a throne for the invisible Yahweh. The association of the bull with Semitic fertility cults however made the use of this figure dangerous to Yahwism. Linked chronologically to the events of Sinai the story heightens Israel's wickedness in spurning the God who had so recently admitted her to special favors. The narrative serves still another purpose. Moses' breaking of the stone tablets in wrath over his people's conduct necessitated a second conference of commandments by Yahweh. Thus the redactor had an opportunity to utilize the Ritual Decalogue (Ex 34:14–26), which could not be fitted in the traditions of Ex 19–24.

According to Ex 19:1 the Hebrews arrived at the Sinai desert three months after their departure from Egypt. Here they remained after the great theophany until "the second year, on the twentieth day of the second month" (Nm 10:11), when they moved on into the desert of Pharan toward the plains of Moab. Preliminary successes over Sehon, Arad, Og and the Madianites (Nm 21 and 31) are portents of the successful conquest of the promised land. Nevertheless the spirit of revolt among the people occasioned a severe sentence from the Lord:

Forty days you spent in scouting the land; forty years shall you suffer for your crimes: one year for each day. Thus you will realize what it means to oppose me. I, the Lord, have sworn to do this to all this wicked community that conspired against me: here in the desert they shall die to the last man (Nm 14:34–35).

Since the conquest of Palestine did not actually follow upon the immediate conclusion of the Exodus the traditions had to explain the delay in the fulfillment of the promise. The murmurings in

95

the desert and during the delay in entering Canaan were regarded as cause and effect. (Dt 7:22 deals with the problem by noting: "He will dislodge these nations before you little by little. You cannot exterminate them all at once, lest the wild beasts become too numerous for you.") Consequently the Israelites are delayed forty years in the plains of Moab until the time decreed by Yahweh for their passage across the Jordan. In this land east of the river the exhortations of Dt have their setting. On the eve of entering into possession of their heritage the people hear a résumé of the deeds of the Lord—deeds which should prompt their grateful response:

Your ancestors went down to Egypt seventy strong, and now the Lord, your God, has made you as numerous as the stars of the sky (Dt. 10:22).

For love of your fathers he chose their descendants and personally led you out of Egypt by his great power, driving out of your way nations greater and mightier than you, so as to bring you in and to make their land your heritage, as it is today (Dt 4:37–38).

The Lord, our God, made a covenant with us at Horeb; not with our fathers did he make this covenant, but with us, all of us who are alive here today (Dt 5:2–3).

The divine mercies elaborated in the Pentateuch prompt loving compliance with the divine will. However, no matter how impressive the deeds of Yahweh are, Israel remains free to reject the claim they make on her. The choice is her own:

I call heaven and earth today to witness against you: I have set before you life and death, the blessing and the curse. Choose life, then, that you and your descendants may live, by loving the Lord, your God, heeding his voice, and holding fast to him. For that will mean life for you, a long life for you to live on the land which the Lord swore he would give to your fathers Abraham, Isaac, and Jacob (Dt 30:19–20).

# Footnotes to Chapter 1

1 The tradition of conquest of the land is sometimes treated as a separate theme, especially by those critics who work with the Hexateuch, since this division includes Jos, in which the promise of the land is fulfilled. For our present purposes the tradition of the promised land will be treated with the promise made to the patriarchs.

2 Elsewhere in the Bible however there are faint allusions to a struggle between Yahweh and the forces of chaos:

You rule over the surging of the sea;
you still the swelling of its waves.
You have crushed Rahab with a mortal blow;
with your strong arm you have scattered your enemies (Ps 89:10–11).

See also Is 51:9; Jb 7:12; 9:13; 25:12; Ps 104:7–9. These texts imply a continuing creativity and a continuous act of divine omnipotence holding in check the forces of chaos.

3 AAS 40 (1948) 47 and RSS, ed Conrad Louis (7th ed, St. Meinrad, Ind. 1962) 152. Re Gn 1–3 read the decree of the Biblical Commission on the historical character of Gn 1–3 (AAS 1 [1909] 567–69 and RSS, 122–24) in the light of the reply made to Cardinal Suhard, ibid, 150–53.

4 Joseph Coppens, "L'interpretation sexuelle du péché du Paradis," ETL 24 (1948) 395–439, endeavors to show that the western Fathers generally regard the transgression of Adam and Eve as sexual, some of them even holding that their sin was the normal use of sex.

Robert Gordis, "The Knowledge of Good and Evil in the Old Testament and in the Qumran Scrolls," JBL 76 (1957) 123–38, asserts that sexual consciousness is the only meaning of knowledge of good and evil which fits all the biblical passages where the term occurs.

5 Although the same verb is used in both members of v 15b, some critics seek to substantiate a judgment of final victory for man by the relative positions of the man and the serpent: standing above the serpent, man is able to deal a mortal blow on the head, whereas the serpent can only attack his adversary on the heel. Given the physical structure of both man and the serpent however it is difficult to see how any other position is possible. Other critics offer a syntactic justification for their judgment by translating the connective in a concessive sense: "He will attack your head, while you will be able only to snap at his heel."

The messianic import of this *Protoevangelium* need not concern us here. The application of the text "He shall crush your head, etc." to Mary is a time-honored interpretation which found its way into the Vulgate text, where a feminine subject pronoun, *ipsa,* was substituted for the masculine form.

[6] R.A.F. MacKenzie, "The Divine Soliloquies," CBQ 17 (1955) 277–86, points out that Yahweh's soliloquies—his thinking aloud how he will deal with man—form a kind of literary genre of their own. See also Gn 2:18; 3:22; 6:3; 8:21ff; 11:6ff; and 18:17–19.

[7] There is an ample bibliography of extrabiblical parallels to usages found in the patriarchal narratives: Roger O'Callaghan, "Historical Parallels to Patriarchal Social Customs," CBQ 6 (1944) 391–405; H. H. Rowley, *From Joseph to Joshua: Biblical Traditions in the Light of Archaeology* (London 1950); ibid, "Recent Discoveries and the Patriarchal Age," BJRylL 32 (1949–50) 44–79; and Roland de Vaux, *Ancient Israel: Its Life and Institutions,* tr John McHugh (New York 1961).

[8] Von Rad's attitude to history is well illustrated in his *Old Testament Theology: The Theology of Israel's Historical Traditions,* vol I, tr D. M. G. Stalker (New York 1962). Noth's methodology is best exemplified in *The History of Israel,* tr P. R. Ackroyd (rev ed, New York 1960); and *Überlieferungsgeschichte des Pentateuch* (Stuttgart 1948). For a different approach see John Bright, *A History of Israel* (Philadelphia 1959).

For criticism of Noth, et al see John Bright, *Early Israel in Recent History Writing* (Studies in Biblical Theology 19; London 1956); and G. Ernest Wright, "Archaeology and Old Testament Studies," JBL 77 (1958) 39–55; ibid, "History and the Patriarchs," ExpT 71 (1959–60) 292–96; and von Rad's reply to Wright, ExpT 72 (1960–61) 213–16.

[9] Sara explains Isaac's name in two ways: "God has given me cause for laughter, and whoever hears of it will laugh (*ṣaḥaq*) with me" (Gn 21:6). The notion of laughter associated with Isaac occurs in all three traditions. The Yahwist narrative of the prophecy of Isaac's birth makes much of Sara's laughter on that occasion; see 18:12–15. The word *ṣaḥaq* is used in the Elohist's description of Isaac playing with Ishmael (21:9) and again in the Yahwist account of Isaac fondling Rebecca (26:8). The word also occurs in the Priestly tradition. When Abraham heard the promise of his son's birth he fell prostrate and laughed (17:17). Besides the popular etymology which derives the name of Isaac from *ṣaḥaq,* there is obviously some further association which remains unknown.

[10] Wherever Lot appears he serves as a foil for the more imposing figure of his uncle. Abraham's superiority to his nephew is evident in ch 14; the patriarch frees Lot from the harassment of the four kings. Lot's proposal to give his daughters to the Sodomites (Gn 19:6–9) is one more example of his ineffectiveness. He is not a bad man—he even evokes sympathy at times—but his fearful and temporizing actions contrast unfavorably with those of Abraham. Completely ineffectual against the Sodomites, unable to impress his intended sons-in-law (19:14), he hesitates in the dread moment of God's judgment upon Sodom and has to be led from the doomed city (19:16).

[11] Manfred Lehmann, "Abraham's Purchase of Machphela and Hittite Law," BASOR 129 (1953) 15–18.

[12] The importance of the basic tradition concerning the promise of land can scarcely be exaggerated. The patriarchal history is organically related to it and the originally independent themes of the primitive history and Sinai have been correlated with it. The promised land is *the* great theme of Dt, where it is mentioned an average of about three times in each chapter, except in the legislative core of chs 12–26. The motif of possession of the land is part of the larger theme of inheritance throughout the Bible; see F. Dreyfus, "La thème de l'heritage dans l'Ancien Testament," RScPhTh 42 (1958) 3–49.

[13] Johannes Pedersen, *Israel: Its Life and Culture* tr Mrs. Auslaug Møller and Annie Fausbøll (2 vol, London 1926 and 1940) II, 182–212, has perhaps the best treatment of the Hebrew blessing. The frequent mention of eating to gain strength for the act of blessing (see Gn 27:4, 10, 31) stresses the idea that benediction is much more than an expression of pious wishes; it is a "creation" of the one who blesses and as such it engages all his vital forces.

[14] Stealing the wooden household god—*tᵉrāfîm*—was perhaps more than a spiteful trick on Laban, for the Nuzu tablets reveal that possession of the household gods gave title to the family property.
If Rachel told the truth about her condition (Gn 31:35) then the idols would be defiled by one in her state of impurity (see Lv 15:19)—a neat satire against gods of wood and stone.

[15] John J. Dougherty, "The Origins of Hebrew Religion: A Study in Method," CBQ 17 (1955) 258.

[16] Gerhard von Rad, "Josephsgeschichte and ältere Chokma," *Gesammelte Studien zum Alten Testament* (Munich 1958) 272–73. This book is scheduled to appear in English in early 1965 under the title *Collected Old Testament Studies;* see bibliography.

[17] The classic documentary theory which ruled against Mosaic authorship inevitably led to the rejection of Moses as he appears in the Pentateuch. With no disinterested contemporary reports to guide them, critics employing exclusively literary criticism could only conclude the impossibility of knowing the historical Moses. Recent scholars have returned to a more moderate position; they generally agree that to deny the historical reality of the person of Moses is to render inexplicable the course of Israel's history, her devotion to the law and her fidelity to Yahwism. Having denied the historicity of Moses as he appears in the Pentateuch, critics have been compelled to acknowledge him as an historical figure on the basis of the judgment of subsequent history.

[18] A. M. Dubarle, "La signification du nom de Iahweh," RScPhTh 35 (1951) 3–21.

[19] See von Rad's explanation of a cultic origin for the Sinai tradition, "Das formgeschichtliche Problem des Hexateuch," *Gesammelte Studien,* 20–27. For criticism of von Rad see Artur Weiser, *Introduction to the Old Testament,* tr from 4th ed by Dorothea Brandon (London 1961) 83–99;

and W. Beyerlin, *Herkunft und Geschichte der ältesten Sinaitradition* (Tübingen 1961).

[20] The sacred mountain (called Sinai by the Yahwist and Priestly writers, Horeb by the Elohist and Deuteronomist) is commonly located in the south of the Sinai peninsula. On the evidence of Ex 3 and Ex 18 however some scholars place it in the land of Madian, i.e. southwestern Arabia. The mention of Horeb in the theophany to Moses (Ex 3:1ff) may be an addition, and it is possible that Ex 18 (which does not actually name the mountain) may be misplaced in the narrative. To locate the mountain in Arabia intensifies the difficulty of reconstructing the itinerary of the Exodus.

## 2

# Pentateuchal Law and Its Relation to the Covenant

### Old and new concepts of biblical law

THE common ancient view of Pentateuchal legislation was quite forthright: the law, granted at Sinai in all its plenitude and unchangeability, was a divine corpus mediated by Moses. Phrases such as "Then God said to Moses" or "Tell the people" were taken literally.

The difficulties that attend the notion of Mosaic law as a static collection given to men in a single stroke of divine revelation are slowly being resolved by modern criticism. And although the tradition of Moses as lawgiver is so clear and compelling that it cannot be ignored, there is much literary evidence—e.g. repetitions, contradictions, linguistic and stylistic differences—attesting that law in the Pentateuch, far from being a coherent, unified corpus promulgated by a single authority, was a gradually evolving body of disparate legislation changing according to milieu and circumstance. The Biblical Commission's reply to Cardinal Suhard expresses well the progressive nature of the law: "There is no one today who . . . refuses to admit a progressive development in the Mosaic laws due to social and religious conditions of later times."[1]

The establishment of chronology however is but one element,

and hardly the most important, in the reconstruction of an accurate picture of biblical law. It is of far greater significance to ascertain the role of law in the relations between Yahweh and Israel. No one doubts that the legislative will of the Lord was operative in earliest Yahwism; the question is: how did Israel understand this will in the various phases of her religious existence? In other words how did Israel regard the law in relation to her alliance with Yahweh? Nineteenth century critics, concerned with the historical problem of final legislative redactions, never asked these fundamental questions. While admitting the great age of certain legal passages they nonetheless assumed that law meant for the early Hebrew community just what it meant for fifth century Judaism—and for nineteenth century Europeans— so that they endowed all law, regardless of the time of its origin, with the characteristics of postexilic legislation. Only lately has the Wellhausen assumption of postexilic origins for law been proven erroneous, and the validity of the Wellhausen thesis limited to those literary creations which embodied the old traditions of law.

How the Israelite tribal community regarded law and its binding force is not completely clear; yet it is safe to say that for the early Hebrews law was not the absolute it became in later Judaism. Law assumed its position of pre-eminence in Hebrew religion only when postexilic reformers sought to bind Israel anew to Yahweh; the law became the *raison d'être* of the Pentateuch, with the narrative sections supplying an historical framework for divine legislation. Judaic emphasis on law is illustrated by the fact that torah, or law, was eventually applied to the entire collection of Pentateuchal writings, even though only about half the books are of a legislative nature. (Torah connotes more than a legal corpus of course.) Religion was equated with fulfillment of the law; obedience was stressed as a condition for membership in the covenant; in short, Yahweh was regarded

102

above all as a legislator to be honored and obeyed. To identify late Judaic attitudes toward law with those of early Israel is to misconstrue not only primitive legislation but primitive Yahwism as well, for such identification imposes a legalism which did not actually characterize it.

These two misconceptions can be rectified by emphasizing the legislative aspects best calculated to bring out the original significance of law in Israel and to show the relation of law to the covenant at the heart of Yahwism. The present chapter will first consider ancient Near Eastern law in general and Israelite dependence upon it; then specifically Israelite characteristics of law resulting from the covenant; and finally the principal law codes found in the Pentateuch. Since our concern is with the primitive significance of Hebrew law we can simplify the task by eliminating from the discussion postexilic legislation. True, all laws are attributed to Moses, and if one reads the Priestly writings uncritically—e.g. the account of the Tent and its furnishings (Ex 25–31) or the ritual of sacrifices (Lv 1–7)—one assumes that the writer is describing customs and usages contemporaneous with the Exodus. Such was the common view until the discovery that these passages are a postexilic return to origins, a retrojection made in the interests of securing greater force and authority for the usages of the second Temple.[2] The same motive prompted the redaction of some ancient laws; it was probably the Priestly writer who, in underlining the importance of the Sabbath for the postexilic community, added motivation to the third command of the Decalogue in Ex 20:8. Faithful to Mosaic origins he preserved the primitive rites and initiated new ones in the spirit of Moses. In any case it is fairly easy to determine the Priestly legislation. Where the writer employed older corpora (perhaps originally independent), he frequently set them off by introductions or subscriptions which expedite their separation from the context. Nm 6:13 for instance begins: "This is

103

the ritual for the Nazirite: . . . ;" and Lv 11:46 ends: "This is the ritual for holocausts. . . ." These additions, often a redactor's professional directives for priests, facilitate the separation of the original law, which is often much older than the explanatory additions. Likewise can the late Priestly legislation be so distinguished; these writings were incorporated into a "Pentateuch" then approaching definitive form, and hence they suffered none of the changes and accretions which complicate the task of establishing ancient law in its primitive form.

### Ancient Near Eastern law in general

The omission of late Priestly law still leaves a sizable collection of legislation to be analyzed. A primary consideration in tracing the origin and development of early biblical law is the influence of non-Israelite sources. Once the myth of Israel's isolation from her neighbors was dispelled scholars soon recognized the agency of nearby peoples in the formation of Hebrew legislation. Here particularly does the close resemblance of some legal stipulations in the Pentateuch to the provisions of codes discovered in the past half century suggest that Israelite law is closely related in its origins to Mesopotamian corpora. Babylon is the richest source of law collections. The oldest, the code of Ur-Nammu, dates from the third dynasty of Ur around 2050. The laws of Eshnunna are a collection of some thirty-eight laws compiled in Akkadian around 1900. From the early post-Sumerian period (1850?) comes the code of King Lipit-Ishtar. The lengthiest of the codes and certainly the best known is that of Hammurabi, carved on a diorite stele at the time of Babylon's expansion around 1725. The Middle Assyrian laws stem from the time of Tiglath-Pileser I in the late twelfth century B.C., but some of their provisions are as old as the fifteenth century. The Hittite laws, written between 1450 and 1200, comprise several closely related although not identical collections. The latest code is that of the neo-Babylonians from the time of Ashurbanipal in the seventh century.

From the bulky legal material of the Pentateuch six codes have been singled out and assigned to one of the traditional documentary sources. Since the separation of the Pentateuchal strands is made chiefly on the basis of the narratives many critics think it arbitrary to reconstruct Hebrew legislation in terms of the classic sources. On what basis for example is it asserted that the Code of the Covenant is the work of the Elohist, or that the Yahwist is responsible for the Ritual Decalogue? For convenience however the customary assignation to sources has here been followed. The Decalogue occurs twice: Ex 20:2–17 (E) and the expanded form of Dt 5:6–21. The Elohist Code of the Covenant, Ex 20:22—23:19, follows the Elohist Decalogue. The Ritual Decalogue of Ex 34:14–26 is part of the Yahwist tradition. Appropriate introductory and concluding chapters set off the Deuteronomic Code of Dt 12–26. The Priestly tradition is represented by the Law of Holiness, Lv 17–26. The obvious similarities between ordinances in the Pentateuchal codes and decrees in the Mesopotamian corpora show the necessity of studying the extrabiblical codes for a better understanding of Israelite law. The following decrees concerning a goring ox illustrate the resemblances:

### The Code of Eshnunna

If an ox gores an(other) ox and causes (its) death, both ox owners shall divide (among themselves) the price of the live ox and also the equivalent of the dead ox.

If the ox is known to gore habitually and the authorities have brought this fact to the knowledge of its owner, but he does not have the ox dehorned, it gores a man and causes (his) death, then the owner of the ox shall pay two-thirds of a mina of silver.

If it gores a slave and causes his death, he shall pay fifteen shekels of silver.[3]

## The Code of Hammurabi

If an ox, when it is walking along the street, gored a seignior to death, that case is not subject to claim.

If a seignior's ox was a gorer, but he did not pad its horns (or) tie up his ox and that ox gored to death a member of the aristocracy, he shall give one-half mina of silver.

If it was a seignior's slave, he shall give one-third mina of silver.[3]

## Ex 21:28–32, 35, 36

When an ox gores a man or woman to death, the ox must be stoned; its flesh may not be eaten. The owner of the ox, however, shall go unpunished. But if the ox was previously in the habit of goring people and its owner, though warned, would not keep it in; should it then kill a man or woman, not only must the ox be stoned, but its owner also must be put to death. If, however, a fine is imposed on him, he must pay in ransom for his life whatever amount is imposed on him. This law applies if it is a boy or a girl that the ox gores. But if it is a male or female slave that it gores, he must pay the owner of the slave thirty shekels of silver, and the ox must be stoned. . . .

When one man's ox hurts another's ox so badly that it dies, they shall sell the live ox and divide this money as well as the dead animal equally between them. But if it was known that the ox was previously in the habit of goring and its owner would not keep it in, he must make full restitution, an ox for an ox; but the dead animal he may keep.

Present knowledge of law in the ancient Near East depends upon the limited number of records preserved; doubtless future archeological discoveries will render this knowledge less tentative. Nevertheless the extant codes, covering more than a millennium, make it possible to sketch a provisional theory of law in the Near East. The word "code" reveals the nature of the collections; they are not original pronouncements promulgated by

106

a ruler or by an official legislative body, but legal procedures collected—that is, codified—to serve for future reference in the administration of justice. Although the laws were issued under royal authority the king did not claim to have formulated the prescriptions himself. Hammurabi for example sees himself as the king of justice to whom Shamash committed law "to cause justice to prevail in the land, to destroy the wicked and the evil, that the strong might not oppress the weak. . . . When Marduk commissioned me to guide the people aright, to direct the land, I established law and justice in the language of the land."[4] Likewise Lipit-Ishtar wants to establish justice in Sumer and Akkad in accordance with the words of Enlil. At the time of their codification many decrees were already ancient precedents handed down from primitive times. Once established the precedents became custom, and custom among the ancients had the force of law. The decrees now available only in codified form had their original life setting in oral decisions delivered in the normal jurisdiction of tribal leaders or elders. Each decision described an appropriate judgment for specific circumstances; when a situation recurred a suitable verdict could be found in the example of an earlier case. Since written codes are the culmination of age-old oral decisions an exclusively literary criticism can never determine their origins.

## The nature of ancient law

The identification of ancient law with techniques or procedures points up a notable difference from the present concept of law. To the modern western mind decrees are more than patterns for decisions; they are stipulations which actually determine court procedure. The Semitic concept of law however, like the Semitic concept of history, cannot be judged by modern standards. Scholars now agree that ancient codes cannot be considered an authoritative, positive law which binds a judge in his interpretation and judgment of a case. Judging from their language, the concept of law in its modern connotation was scarcely developed among the Babylonians and Assyrians. Entirely lacking are such expressions as "observe the law," "disobey the law" or "judged according to the law." Hammurabi's code, though presented as a code for judges, is silent on punishment for nonobservance. Moreover the numerous contracts and letters of the time are singularly lacking in references to law, thus posing again the question of the role of law and its relation to juridic practice. But if the law imposed no binding obligation what purpose did it serve? Intensive legal studies of recent years have not yet decided the precise import of the codes; therefore the answer must remain more or less conjectural. Some corpora might have been the private composition of scribes and thus without direct effect upon social life and juridic practice. Codification may have resulted from significant changes in the political order: a new dynasty, notable expansion or revolution. The codified precedents would thus be available as patterns of conduct in the new regime. At least three of the codes could have arisen under such conditions: the laws of Ur-Nammu at the start of the third dynasty of Ur, the code of Hammurabi in the period of Babylonian expansion and the Hittite code in the transitional period between the old and new empires. The establishment of the monarchy may have been the occasion for the codification of Israel's early laws. We will discuss this problem at greater length when we examine the specific nature of Hebrew law.

Another puzzling problem is how the peoples of Mesopotamia came to share a common legal heritage. Several solutions have been proposed: perhaps there existed a primitive legal corpus from which later codes derived; perhaps the peoples shared a common legal heritage. The origin of Hebrew law is especially difficult to establish. Upon their entrance into Canaan the Israelites must have possessed at least an oral law, possibly influenced by laws of the eighteenth dynasty in Egypt. In fact the Book of Judges is inexplicable without a tradition vital enough to resist absorption into Canaan. In the absence of texts however we can only speculate. Because of Israel's close relations with Canaan after the settlement in Palestine it is reasonable to look to the Canaanites for early influences on Hebrew law. There is however a problem. Although a consensus of scholars admits Canaanite influence, no Canaanite code of law has been found; hence verification of Hebrew dependence is as yet impossible. Even if Canaanite influence was admitted as an hypothesis, without the original documents we cannot know the process of adaption. Was Canaanite law first taken over by a single tribe and later extended, or did it apply to the tribal federation from the beginning? Such considerations as the simpler structure of the Israelite "state" would require alteration of the borrowed material, but the particular changes made and the criteria dictating them cannot be singled out. And perhaps the question has received disproportionate emphasis; was Canaanite law really so different from the rest of Mesopotamian legislation? Even if we do not know the factors which shaped early biblical legislation we can at least be sure that the development of Hebrew law was not a strictly internal process occurring in isolation from neighboring countries. Mesopotamian law exercised marked influence on Hebraic law, but the exact sources, time and extent of the influence are at present indeterminable.

## Hebrew law

### Its redactive nature

The legislation Israel assimilated from Mesopotamian neighbors occurs in codes far removed from their primary sources. The growth of Israelite law and its redaction to meet changed conditions make it obvious that biblical decrees are the final stage

109

of a protracted process; nowhere do they appear in original form. To this proposition both literary and form critics agree. By the time the codes were introduced into the Pentateuch the original sources were probably no longer available to the redactor, who had to work with intermediate collections already constituted. The redactive nature of law accounts for repetitions within the same corpus, e.g. Lv 18:6–30 and 20:10–26. The redactor was bound by his material in the legislative sections no less than in the narrative—a defect from a literary or esthetic viewpoint but a boon to critical analysis.

Laws with so complex a history have prompted many studies. The initial step in analysis is the removal of the legislation from the narratives in which it is imbedded. Traditional literary criticism then proceeds to separate laws according to stylistic differences. Form criticism pursues the analysis further and by comparison with extrabiblical legislation and by determination of the life setting endeavors to trace the received law to its origins —a hazardous and frequently impossible undertaking. Assigning dates to the origins of laws and to the various stages of their development is likewise a parlous task, though one which did not greatly concern nineteenth century scholars, whose interest in chronology was confined to establishing when the codes appeared in their definitive forms. The newer concept of J, E, D and P as pliant currents of tradition has made the dating of documents less significant, but modern critics have a chronological inquisitiveness of their own. Recent critical studies of the time and origin of the component elements of a code have added in no small measure to a more accurate interpretation of law and religion. It should be noted however that excessive preoccupation with individual components also has dangers; concentration on isolated elements can atomize the Pentateuch quite as effectively as exaggerated source criticism can. Israel's traditions must always be treated as a whole.

110

## Casuistic and apodictic law

Biblical legal terminology gives only meager clues to the nature and kinds of Hebrew law. The commandments of the Decalogue are literally "the ten words" ($d^e b\bar{a}r\hat{\imath}m$). The preface to the Code of the Covenant states: "These are the rules ($mi\check{s}p\bar{a}t\hat{\imath}m$) you shall lay before them" (Ex 21:1). The favorite expressions in Dt are "statutes and decrees" ($huqq\hat{\imath}m\ w^e mi\check{s}p\bar{a}t\hat{\imath}m$) or "statutes and commandments" ($huqq\hat{\imath}m\ w^e misw\bar{o}t$). Dt 4:45 speaks of "the ordinances, statutes, and decrees" ($h\bar{a}'ed\bar{o}t\ w^e hahuqq\hat{\imath}m\ w^e hammi\check{s}p\bar{a}t\hat{\imath}m$) Moses proclaimed to the people. Dt 4:44 specifies: "This is the law ($hatt\hat{o}r\hat{a}$) which Moses set before the Israelites." The Priestly legislation uses '$ed\hat{u}t,$ from the same root as witness. The process is not entirely clear but it seems that the Priestly writer regards the laws as permanent signs meant to recall the basic Sinai covenant. Although these terms differ in their primitive connotations they are used in the Pentateuch with more or less the same meaning. Therefore any conclusion on Hebrew law that is based on the legal terms employed is conjectural.

In analysis of biblical law no one has surpassed Albrecht Alt (1883–1956), whose distinction of the kinds of Hebrew law, though not universally accepted, has clarified the nature and origin of Israelite legislation. According to Alt biblical legislation falls into two categories: casuistic and apodictic. The distinction is not original but he was the first to conclude that apodictic law is specifically Israelite in origin.[5] Casuistic ordinances are the techniques or cases already described in the extrabiblical codes; such laws Israel possessed in common with her neighbors. On the other hand apodictic laws—categorical, unconditional decrees—seem distinctively and exclusively Israelite. A casuistic formula details the action to be taken in a particular situation: "When a man gives money or any article to another for safekeeping and it is stolen from the latter's house, the thief, if caught, must make twofold restitution" (Ex 22:6). Stylistically speaking an introductory "when" or "if" characterizes case law, and since definite circumstances are described the sentence is longer and more periodic than is usual in Hebrew. There is general agreement on the "lay" nature of hypothetical law; official lawyers are lacking, the priesthood is not mentioned and the realm of sacral law is scarcely touched upon. Addressed to a sedentary people the early casuistic formulas reflect the village or tribe of premonarchic Israel as the basic social unit.

Apodictic law differs from casuistic prescriptions both in structure and in content. The casuistic formula in Ex 21:13–14 states: "He, however, who did not hunt a man down, but caused his death by an act of God, may flee to a place which I shall set apart for this purpose. But when a man kills another after maliciously scheming to do so, you must take him even from my altar and put him to death." The categorical decree of Ex 20:13 reads: "You shall not kill." Here the validity of the law is independent of the conditions attached to hypothetical legislation. The apodictic formula forbids killing; it does not distinguish between murder and homicide, between objective and subjective guilt; it makes no provision for blood vengeance or asylum. Such unqualified, categorical formulation is the stamp of true apodictic law.

Usually apodictic legislation is expressed in the second person plural, although this structure is not essential. Apodictic law also includes the participial formulations found chiefly in the Code of the Covenant, e. g. "Whoever strikes a man a mortal blow must be put to death" (Ex 21:12). In translation the passage loses the distinctive flavor of the original and does not appear too different from the hypothetical clauses which follow. The terseness of the apodictic formula is clearer in Hebrew: "*Makkēh 'iš, wāmēt, môt yûmāt.*" Here the offense, the consequence and the

112

judgment are covered—all in five words. The Decalogues of Ex 20:7–17 and Dt 5:6–21 as well as the curses of Dt 27:14–26 are made up solely of apodictic decrees. But most apodictic laws were probably not transmitted as formed corpora; rather they were inserted at an early date into a primary text of hypothetical decrees, thus gaining force beyond what they originally possessed as isolated data. The combination is exemplified in Ex 21:12—23:9 where apodictic participial formulas are interspersed with casuistic laws treating the same matter. Sometimes a single law combines both apodictic and casuistic styles. In Ex 21:23 for example the "if" characteristic of hypothetical statutes opens the verse: "But if injury ensues, . . ." Then the style reverts to the apodictic formulation in the *lex talionis:* "You shall give life for life, eye for eye, tooth for tooth, hand for hand, foot for foot, burn for burn, wound for wound, stripe for stripe." The verse betrays two laws differing in their roots, each with its own history of oral transmission before being united in a single decree.

The probable derivation of Hebrew case law from Israel's neighbors has been noted. The question now arises: what is the origin of apodictic law? The absence of categorical formulas in the extrabiblical codes strongly suggests that apodictic decrees are specifically Israelite; one need not look beyond Israel for their origin.[6] Moreover the structure and content of categorical laws seem to demand that their origin be sought in Yahwism itself. Their provenance could have been a cultic center where legal series in categorical style developed for liturgical use in commemoration of the covenant with Yahweh. Josue's gathering of all Israel at Sichem for covenant renewal (Jos 24:1ff) may be just such an occasion. (It is true however that apodictic law is not mentioned in the account of Josue's assembly. There are several alternative explanations for this lack: perhaps ch 24 is no longer in its original context, or in a curtailed form. At one time the passage on covenant renewal may have been a frame for a law corpus such as the Code of the Covenant.) If Josue's assembly is an isolated event no conclusion on apodictic law as a specific form can be drawn, since only through repetition in a people's life do the structure and content of a literary form acquire consistency. The frequent recurrence of covenantal assemblies can be posited with some probability however since Moses left instructions for the preservation and reading of the law (Dt 31:9–13). In addition the structures of Dt 27:14–26 and the Decalogue—both definitely associated with the inauguration of the covenant—are well suited to liturgical usage and could readily fit into a life setting like that of Jos 24.

## Law and the covenant

### Nature of the covenant bond

The theory that apodictic law is exclusively Israelite in origin has not yet been fully validated. We are much more sure of the close connection between law and covenant. Scholars disagree on the origin of the concept of alliance with Yahweh, yet they all admit the covenantal nature of Israel's religion. Election by Yahweh is a fact—the core of Hebrew religion. Since this fact found expression in the legal form of the covenant a discussion of Hebrew law is incomplete without an examination of the basic covenantal structure which produced and supported it. The passages in the Pentateuch employing the word "covenant" help clarify the life setting and the procedures of the compact. Abraham made a covenant with Abimelech, giving him seven ewe lambs as proof that Abraham's men had dug the wall at Bersabee (Gn 21:22–32). The pact was concluded by both men taking an oath. At Galaad Jacob and Laban erected a heap of stones and with God as witness promised not to pass with evil intent beyond this rock border (Gn 31:44–53). The new relation between Jacob and Laban was based on their agreement and on the mutual obligations it imposed. Covenants of a different sort are those of Yahweh with Noe (Gn 9:8–17) and with Abraham (Gn 15:9–20) in which Yahweh imposed no specific obligations, but only promised never again to destroy mankind by a flood and to increase Abraham's posterity. The mysterious rites accompanying the alliance with Abraham were probably ceremonies of ratification attached to all covenants. The Priestly writer's distinctive use of the covenant concept will be treated later.

Although these biblical passages embody various elements of the covenant they provide only a partial picture of the legal institution involved in the Sinai alliance. More complete parallels to the covenant with Yahweh can be found in the Hittite suzerainty (unilateral) treaties binding vassals to their king. The treaty records of the Hittites between 1450 and 1200 are the best source for legal procedures which may also have been current in Israel.[7] The establishment of mutual support between the contracting parties is the principal aim of the treaty. Since the agreement is unilateral the vassal's oath of obedience entails no corresponding promise from the king; *noblesse oblige* assures the sovereign's protection of his subjects. The treaties do not follow a rigid scheme, but the same elements, in different order and wording, are common to all of them. A preamble identifies the initiator of the covenant; an historical prologue then reviews the situation between the two parties. The heart of the treaty details the obligations placed upon the vassal. A fourth section provides that the document be stored in the temple and read periodically to the people. The two final sections list the divine witnesses and the curses or blessings to follow upon rebellion or obedience. Ratification of the treaty no doubt involved other factors, such as solemn rites accompanying the vassal's promises of obedience; but of these ceremonies nothing is known with certainty.

Since descriptions of covenants in the Pentateuch lack the completeness and precision of the Hittite documents the treaties might seem of little use in understanding Yahweh's alliance with Israel. The structure and content of the Hittite pacts can nonetheless help identify those biblical traditions which preserve isolated elements of the Sinai covenant. The curses of Dt 27 for instance, obviously out of place, may have once formed part of an elaborate covenantal record. In the light of Hittite patterns many elements of covenantal structure can be detected in the Ex account of the alliance, which relates how the mixed multitude leaving Egypt was shaped by the covenant into a community enjoying solidarity and status. The narrative of deliverance from Egypt and the consequent obligations to Yahweh form the historical prelude. The text of the covenantal stipulations is the Decalogue, to which the community promises obedience: "When Moses came to the people and related all the words and ordinances of the Lord, they all answered with one voice, 'We will do everything that the Lord has told us'" (Ex 24:3; see also 19:8). The reading of the "Book of the Covenant" and the sprinkling of blood upon the altar are evidently part of the ratification ceremonies.

It might be noted parenthetically that Jos 24 bears the closest resemblance to the pattern of the Hittite treaties. An introductory formula states: "Thus says the Lord, the God of Israel" (Jos 24:2a); a citation of past benefits follows in vv 2b–13. There is only one covenantal stipulation: that foreign gods be cast aside (vv 14–15); it is mentioned however that further statutes and ordinances were recorded and preserved (vv 25–26). Witnesses to the covenant are the people themselves and the memorial stones they set up (vv 22 and 27). The customary formulas of blessings and curses are not listed.

In reconstructing the Sinai tradition Gerhard von Rad arranges

116

the pericopes of Ex and Dt in a pattern resembling the treaties in question: [8]

Ex 19–24

    1 Exhortation and presentation of the background of Sinai events.

    2 Presentation of law (Decalogue and Code of the Covenant).

    3 Promise of blessings.

    4 Ratification of the covenant.

Dt 1–27

    1 History of events at Sinai and exhortation.

    2 Presentation of law.

    3 Ratification of the covenant

    4 Blessings and curses.

## The covenantal context of Hebrew law

Martin Noth's studies of the Israelite tribal federation, the amphictyony, have shed additional light on the relation between law and covenant. Israelite history, Noth makes clear, begins only with the tribal settlement in Palestine; but the traditions of prehistoric Israel profoundly influenced that settlement and gave rise to a prepolitical confederation of tribes bound by covenant to Yahweh and centered in a cultic shrine. For Noth all of Israelite history is bound up with this amphictyony, and the importance of his studies on the subject can hardly be overestimated.[9] If Noth is correct then the amphictyony is an institution which can serve as a connective between countless Old Testament elements which older criticism understood only as a part of a preconceived evolutionary schematism.

Nonetheless two criticisms can be noted. That a tribal federation existed is not doubted; see for example 3 Kgs 12:16: "What portion have we in David? Or what inheritance in the son of Isai? Go home to thy dwellings, O Israel. Now, David, look to thy own house. So Israel departed to their dwellings." In view of the scanty evidence however Noth carries his hypothesis too far in

117

attributing to the covenant characteristics of the later Greek amphictyony. Moreover the Hebrew federation was modified much more sharply with the passage of time than Noth indicates. And although Noth correctly names the covenant as the basis of the amphictyony and the chief presupposition of Israelite law, he tends to regard it as man-initiated, a device of human contrivance in the interests of political union. But the covenant is essentially the work of Yahweh, and is a source of constant wonder to Israel and a challenge to total commitment.

The foremost tradition of the amphictyony was that of Yahweh as the God of Israel, whose alliance with the community was grounded in historical events of long ago. Thus from earliest times Israel associated her constitution as a people with the free choice and covenant of the Lord. The bond was not simply a union which gave expression to national religious sentiments by worship of Yahweh; on the contrary the union existed only because the will of Yahweh had effected it. Like its later Greek and Roman counterparts the amphictyony was subject to divine legislation, which, Noth insists, was in no sense a state law; it did not create but presumed an already existing order—that of a covenantal society—which it was to protect.

Without parallel in the Near East, the covenantal structure of Israel's religion and society made of Hebrew law a thing apart. It is true that throughout the ancient law codes the distinction between *ius* (strictly legal prescriptions) and *fas* (general moral commands) was not accurately made. All ancient law is to some degree theocratic and religious interests predominate even in profane matters; yet the nature and extent of this religious pervasion of law is unique in Israel. If we seek to establish what distinguishes Mosaic law from similar ancient legislation we find it in the force with which the entire Hebrew law was linked to Yahweh. Despite their dependence on a divine legislator the extrabiblical codes remain essentially secular, whereas biblical law is an integral part of Israel's religion. Other peoples have looked upon their divinities as parents or masters but the link binding gods and men was always natural and necessary, not one of free choice. The God of Israel on the other hand voluntarily initiated an alliance between his people and himself. Unlike the other gods who could only guarantee the law and commission its promulgation Yahweh, having first chosen a people for himself, revealed to them the principles assuring the preservation of their election. Since the divine will was operative in instituting the covenant the same will decreed the law by which Israel could maintain herself in the alliance. This concept of law as a direct revelation of God is peculiar to Israel; all the corpora, except the addresses of Moses in Dt, are presented as utterances of Yahweh.

Further Yahweh's complete transcendence over all creation demands, once he has chosen to make an alliance with the work of his hands, that men in some way partake of the divine transcendence, and this fact introduces a certain tension, a certain ambivalence into Israel's relations with the Lord. Although the Pentateuchal traditions use anthropomorphisms freely (the covenant itself is one vast anthropomorphism), there is at the same time a profound realization of the opposition between the human and the divine. Yahweh is the Totally Other with whom man cannot communicate as he does with his fellowmen. What is holy is foreign to the creature; it simultaneously terrifies, repulses and attracts him.[10] Drawn by covenant into intimate communion with the Holy One, Israel could no longer live in a purely secular realm. All of life was marked with the grace of the covenant. In the final analysis then Hebrew law is unique because Yahweh and Yahwism are unique.

Thus Israel brought all legislation—that which she borrowed from her neighbors and that of her own creation—to the service of religion in extending Yahweh's controlling influence over

119

the whole of life. She assimilated the secular law around her and brought it gradually within the ambit of Sinai, where Yahweh had established his covenant and decreed his law for Israel. The parallels between biblical and extrabiblical codes do not necessarily mean that there is little distinction between them. Israel took over the form and content of Mesopotamian legislation but the spirit of Yahwism permeated the borrowed law and made of it a new creation.

So dependent is legislation on the alliance with Yahweh that biblical law cannot be interpreted apart from the covenant which is its foundation and support. The purpose of the law is preservation of the covenant; lawbreaking is betrayal of the covenant. From earliest days Israel's cult stressed the will of Yahweh expressed in commands like those of the Decalogue. Obviously the ordinances exact obedience and their infraction entails sanctions. One cannot conclude however that the relation between Yahweh and Israel is fundamentally a legal one, as if observance of the law constituted the Hebrews God's people. Rather Yahweh's election of Israel is prior to the commands laid upon her. By the will of the Lord, Israel was made a special people with as yet no laws to dictate the terms of her relation to Yahweh. Her status as a chosen nation was of course morally conditioned and inseparable from certain norms.[11] Obedience is a prerequisite of salvation but observance alone cannot save. Israel recognized and practiced this truth from the start in much the same way that the early Christian community, though conscious that it was no longer "under the law," obeyed the moral commandments. The question is a matter of emphasis. The covenant required obedience to law but its chief demand was for commitment, total dedication to Yahweh. Law was never an end in itself. If Israel will fix her gaze upon the Lord, ponder his works in her behalf, commit herself in gratitude to him, then observance of the law will follow as a matter of course. Such is the burden of the Deuteronomic presentation of law; the preacher enjoins observance of "the statutes, decrees, and ordinances" in the context of love and gratitude to Yahweh, who has favored Israel by his covenant.

It was divorce from the covenant which led eventually to the conception of law as an absolute. Israelite law lost its covenantal basis when all traces of the amphictyony vanished with the last of the Judean kings in 587. No hope remained for the restoration of the federation even though a new covenant, set in an eschatological framework, was awaited. Law however could be preserved. An exiled people desirous of preserving religious identity had greater need than did a people living on its own soil for a definite moral norm other than personal whim. Divinely revealed law provided the norm. The unstable conditions of the Exile forced Israel to adjust and interpret the ancient traditions anew. In many ways the Exile resembled the time when Moses the legislator was active: the people was again without state and territory; the conditions of Egyptian bondage and desert sojourn had parallels in the life of enforced exile. And as Moses had legislated for this period so did men of the new age build upon the ancient foundations a law which could carry Israel into the future, when she would repossess her land in peace and security.

Since law alone remained to mark a man as a Jew, ordinances like the Sabbath observance and circumcision took on added significance and were given an earlier date of foundation. And as we noted above, the concern to establish primitive bases for legal observances dictated much of the Priestly writing. Once law had been separated from the covenant then other alliances could be stressed: those with Noe and Abraham, and even the so-called Davidic covenant. Thus during and after the Exile the divine protection guaranteed by Israel's election was linked to the law conceived as an absolute. Priests assumed a greater part in expounding the law; godly, practical men labored for

121

the establishment of a community whose holiness lay in scrupulous legal observance. Detached from the covenant, law was judged to be the eternal expression of the divine will revealed by special privilege to Israel. Small wonder then that such reflections led to a cult of the law. The later current of Hebrew wisdom literature promoted the concept of law as an absolute by the identification of the law with wisdom. Nevertheless the true spirit of the law, depicted most forcibly by the Deuteronomist, was never wholly lost to view.[12]

## Biblical codes individually considered

### The Decalogue

Having noted the origin, nature and purpose of Hebrew law, we can now turn to individual codes. Among the Pentateuchal corpora the Decalogue—the ten words of Ex 20:2–17 and Dt 5:6–21—enjoys pre-eminence, and with good reason. Presented as the oldest direct revelation of Yahweh, the decrees lie at the heart of the Sinai tradition and, no matter how interpreted, they play a significant role in the covenant contracted between Yahweh and Israel through the mediation of Moses. The categoric sentences in the series pertain to most of the dimensions of moral behavior; perhaps this emphasis on morality explains the worldwide adoption and influence of the Ten Commandments. Philosophy has accepted them as an explication of the natural law common to all men, and Christianity has retained the tradition of God's revelation of the commands.

Given the exalted position of the Ten Commandments as the vehicle of Yahweh's revelation, it may be surprising to discover that the form and content of the Decalogue are not unique; one may in fact speak of a decalogue as a literary form.

Since the number ten is convenient for counting, very likely a decalogue structure was frequently used in the oral stages of Israel's traditions. Lv 19 for instance can be divided into two decalogues, one singular, the other plural. Other possible examples of decalogue structure are found in Ex 18, Dt 27 and Ex 34. The instances available suggest that the form originated in the cultic instructions given worshippers participating in a feast. The "catechisms" employed were both cultic (Ex 34:14–26) and ethical, as in the Ten Commandments. Instruction given in the sanctuaries was related to the priestly oracles and later to the priestly torah, or instruction in the law. Despite the general agreement of scholars on the genesis of the decalogue form, confirmatory evidence is not yet available; therefore the cultic origin and development of the Decalogue remain problematic.

After long years of oral transmission entailing changes and additions, certain decalogues became part of written Hebrew literature. Some of them were incorporated with other legal matter; others—like the ten words—retained their identity as individual corpora. In either event the received versions differ from the primitive form of the oral tradition. In other words the primitive laws are not directly at the base of the decalogues as they now appear, and it is doubtful that the original forms will ever be known.

Some conjectures about the Ten Commandments can nonetheless be made. The great age of the Decalogue is evident from the fact that it is treated as authoritative in both E and D. Language and structure show that the E Decalogue is the older of the two. From the negative formulation of almost all the commands in both versions it is assumed by some scholars that the stipulations of parental obedience and Sabbath observance were originally negative also. The motivation added to the third and fourth commands is the work of Deuteronomic and Priestly redactors, but the lateness of the additions is no argument against the age of the primitive code.

At this point the question might be raised: if the decalogues originated in primitive cultic observances and developed as oral traditions, is not the attribution of Mosaic origin to the Ten Commandments entirely gratuitous? Critics of the last century thought so. The Wellhausen assumption that cultic law develops before moral law was one reason for postulating a late composition for the Decalogue. The absence of references to Moses and his work in the preaching of the prophets also led to skepticism about Moses as legislator for Israel. Today however many scholars consent to the possibility of Mosaic composition. Although absolute proof is lacking it can be demonstrated that the provisions of the Decalogue are both possible and probable in Moses' time. Whatever the age of the commandments there is no doubt of their intimate association with the Sinai covenant so central to the traditions of Yahwism; the peculiar character of the Decalogue derives from its covenantal basis. And for some scholars the Decalogue *is* the covenant stipulating the obligations the community accepts. Though not law, its prescriptions are the source of law, for the community must of course prevent breach of the alliance. Considering the gaps in current knowledge of Hebrew legislation the distinction between Decalogue as covenant and Decalogue as law is perhaps too subtle, but it serves at least to affirm the close relation between the two ideas.

## The Code of the Covenant

As part of the Sinai tradition the Code of the Covenant (Ex 20:22—23:19) follows close upon the Elohist Decalogue. Its name derives from the ceremonies of covenant ratification in

124

Ex 24:3–8, which tells how Moses related to the people "all the words and ordinances of the Lord," then wrote down "all the words of the Lord" and finally, "taking the Book of the Covenant . . . he read it aloud to the people."[13] Despite their presentation as primitive legislation connected with the alliance at Sinai, "all the words and ordinances of the Lord" are not necessarily a direct revelation of Yahweh, nor are they a comprehensive code of unified style, an original composition by Moses. Casuistic laws—and these take up more than half the code— are interspersed with apodictic decrees in both the singular and the plural. There are also participial formulations and combinations of styles treating penal, social, cultic and moral matters. The lack of unity in the conflation implies great variety in the sources used by the redactor. Consequently, although this code is one of the oldest legislative texts of Israel, its present form is by no means primitive; it is an amalgamation of legislative material differing in content, style and time of composition. Perhaps the corpus as found in Ex is not the complete redaction, for there are obvious gaps and omissions. The absence of sexual legislation hints that the code is only a portion of a more comprehensive corpus circulated independently before being incorporated into the Pentateuch. It has been suggested that the sexual laws of Lv 20 may at one time have followed Ex 22:16. But it is also possible that the silence on sexual matters is evidence for the great age of the code, since the more primitive the legislation the less it interferes with family concerns.

Critical studies of the Code of the Covenant abounded in the late nineteenth century, for this collection was seen as a point of departure for tracing the religious evolution of Israel from the law of the altar through Dt to Lv. While admitting the antiquity of some sections of the text, scholars of the last century nevertheless believed that the Covenant Code was a late composition, certainly no earlier than the beginning of the ninth century. Since the discovery of the Mesopotamian codes the trend is toward an earlier date; yet beyond conceding that the collection is very old—definitely preprophetic—critics have not reached agreement as to its age. Catholic scholars generally hold for an early date of composition and for some sections even claim Mosaic authorship; nevertheless they admit that the determination of Mosaic elements is conjectural. Despite the varying facets of the code all the sources involved represent the same type of society: somewhat primitive, strongly familial, with vaguely defined political powers and strong religious traditions. Some parts imply a nomadic or pastoral society; others, agricultural. The combination indicates that the code was drawn up in the transitional period when the Israelites passed from seminomadic to sedentary life in the early days of the tribal amphictyony.

The casuistic laws forming the bulk of the collection suggest an origin in the decisions given by lay judges or tribal leaders; yet the code is by no means secular. Apodictic formulas interwoven with casuistic laws bring the collection under the sway of Yahwism, thus forming a redaction of ancient legislation according to the spirit of its Mosaic origins. Most of the Ten Commandments recur in expanded form, revealing how the redaction is permeated by the spirit of the Decalogue. Even the position of the code in the Sinai narrative accentuates its relation to the covenant as the amphictyonic law promulgated to preserve Israel in her alliance with Yahweh. True, there is little agreement about the original disposition of the legislation in the Sinai pericope of Ex 19–34. As the law of the amphictyony the Code of the Covenant may have been joined at one time to the covenant renewal described in Jos 24. But regardless of its former position, the redactor clearly wished to show its dependence on the Sinai revelation.

126

## The Ritual Decalogue

The third and final corpus fitted into the Sinai narrative is the so-called Ritual Decalogue of Ex 34:14–26. The phrase "so-called" is a necessary modification on two counts: the laws are not exclusively cultic, nor are they easily reduced to the number ten, although critics have devoted much time to rearranging and editing the verses to achieve a satisfactory decalogue structure. That cultic decrees precede moral legislation was a favorite dictum of those who interpreted Israel's religion in Hegelian terms. On this assumption who could doubt that the liturgical prescriptions in Ex 34 are older than the ethical Decalogue? But with the passing of evolutionistic descriptions of Yahwism critics now tend to be less dogmatic in their assertion of cultic priority; ritual legislation and ethical legislation could have been linked together even in early Yahwism.[14] If the Ritual Decalogue is thought to be ancient, it is not cultic emphasis which leads to such a judgment. By reason of vocabulary and style the code is assigned to the Yahwist. Its zeal for the usages of primitive Yahwism and its forceful rejection of alliances outside the sacral community justify the assertion of early composition.

Because of the zealous defense of Yahweh's claim to exclusive worship—apparent in the tone of the code—it is questionable to view the corpus as merely cultic. Explicit liturgical directives are given: "No one shall appear before me empty-handed. . . . You shall keep the feast of Weeks. . . . You shall not offer me the blood of sacrifice with leavened bread" (Ex 34:20, 22, 25). All these instructions however flow from the primordial concern that Yahweh's right to worship be guarded, a right summed up in the commands: "You shall not worship any other god. . . . You shall not make for yourself molten gods" (Ex 34:14, 17). The prohibitions are a coin whose obverse is the positive command of liturgical worship. It is characteristic of Israel's assimilative power that in the very act of fulfilling the command to worship Yahweh exclusively she could freely utilize liturgical forms current among her pagan neighbors, as she no doubt did in certain festal observances.[16]

There are few provisions in the Ritual Decalogue which do not also appear in the ethical Decalogue or in the Covenant Code. Perhaps a redactor jealously devoted to purity of worship assembled (either from the Code of the Covenant or from one of that code's sources) laws pertinent to the worship of Yahweh as prescribed in the first three commands of the ethical Decalogue.

## The Law of Holiness

The assertion that the Priestly writing as a whole is of late composition does not mean that some parts of it are not very old, or even ancient. The dominant purpose of the Priestly redactor was to preserve and give priority to the usages of purest Yahwism, especially in its concepts of divine election, revealed law and sin against the divine commands. Thus it is truly from the spirit of Moses, if not from his time, that the Priestly legislation proceeds. The oldest elements of the Priestly writing are found in the Law of Holiness (Lv 17–26), which was fashioned by joining early independent collections with contemporary additions and interpretations. This composite nature of the Law of Holiness (a term first used by August Klostermann in the nineteenth century) explains why the code echoes the legislation of earlier corpora—the Decalogue, the Code of the Covenant, Ritual Decalogue—as well as that of Dt and other parts of the Priestly tradition. In contrast to the strict unity of Lv 1–7 on sacrificial ritual or of chs 11–16 with their solicitude for legal purity, the Holiness Code at first glance appears to be a haphazard juxtaposition of all sorts of laws:

cultic, social and ethical. What imposes unity on the series is the recurring theme of holiness. When through the covenant the Hebrews were made uniquely Yahweh's own they became a people governed by the moral will of a God who loves good and hates evil. As Yahweh's possession their lives had to show the stamp of the Holy One, who reminds them: "Be holy, for I, the Lord, your God, am holy" (Lv 19:2).

Thus the Law of Holiness legislates for all aspects of life. The encompassing nature of the code illustrates the universal reach of the holiness Yahweh enjoins; no human activity is independent of the directive will of the holy and hallowing Lord. Whereas Lv 11–16 is concerned with one type of holiness, legal purity, the Holiness Code surpasses these narrow limits and emphasizes that sanctity must characterize the whole of man's actions. To convey his teaching the Priestly redactor loosely combined laws touching all phases of activity, altered them according to circumstance and united them by the holiness motif. The refrain "Be holy, for I, the Lord, your God, am holy" is not mechanically distributed; it occurs most frequently in ch 19, which is perhaps the high point of the code, and then occasionally throughout the rest of the legislation. It does not appear at all in chs 20 and 21, which however do contain other admonitions to sanctity. The holiness refrain and the oft-repeated "I am the Lord" of ch 18 prompt the conjecture that some of the formerly independent collections of the Holiness Code originated in cultic sanctuaries, where repetitive responses may have been a part of instruction on the law. Each of the component corpora has layers of its own, a fact most easily recognized in ch 19; here two independent codes have been joined, characterized by the use of the second person plural (vv 3–12) and second person singular (vv 13–18) respectively. The amalgamation of distinct sources betrays itself elsewhere in lesser degree. If the cultic origin of the component codes is

129

granted then it is understandable that the Law of Holiness, although it includes legislation of every kind, should forcibly stress cultic prescriptions.

What can be said of the age of the components and their redaction? The proclivity of the Priestly writer to surround new legislation with the aura of Mosaic origins dictates caution in assigning an early date to laws which seem to have Sinai or the desert as their life setting; yet this caution should not lead to the assertion that none of the prescriptions of the Holiness Code is ancient. The core of the sacrificial law in ch 17 is undoubtedly old; it does not make use of the liturgy of centralized cult (although this position is challenged of course by those who contend that Lv 17:19 legislates for a single altar), and it does not distinguish ritual slaughter from profane slaughter as Dt later does. At present the time of the final conflation is still a disputed question. Similarities in legislation and the exhortatory tone (readily apparent in Lv 18:1–5 and 22–30) imply the influence of Dt. On the other hand resemblances to laws in Ez occasion the opinion that the Law of Holiness is the work of Ezechiel or one of his school. More probably Lv 17–26 was already written in Ezechiel's time; it may have been the scroll (Ez 2:9–10) on which Ezechiel based his reproaches to Israel. Probably the last days of the monarchy saw the codification of the Law of Holiness by the Jerusalem priests, a compilation analogous to that of Dt made in the north. Jerusalem, where Isaia in the eighth century repeatedly denoted Yahweh as "the Holy One of Israel" (Is 6:3), is a fitting provenance for a code which enjoins holiness "because I, Yahweh, am holy."

## The Deuteronomic Code

The Deuteronomic Code, last of the biblical corpora to be considered, is a bold contrast to the other Pentateuchal law collections. As the Greek title signifies, the book repeats and amplifies Israel's traditional laws, enclosing them in a narrative frame which heightens the impression of law as a direct, personal revelation of the Lord on Sinai. Closely resembling the other codes in content but differing radically from them in vocabulary, style and ideology, Dt is literarily independent of the other books of the Pentateuch. Jerome identified Josia as "the justest of men, during whose reign Dt was discovered in the Temple" (PL 23, 217), and critics are generally agreed that Dt is the document found by Helcias during the reign of King Josia (4 Kgs 22:8). (Despite the consensus identifying Dt with Helcias' document some biblical scholars are currently re-examining the nature of the manuscript found in the Temple.) [16]

Martin de Wette proposed in 1805 that Dt is a priestly fraud, a contemporary document masquerading as an ancient composition. The year of its discovery, 621, became the one precise date in the Wellhausen chronology of the documents and nineteenth century criticism leaned heavily on it. The key position of Dt in the four-source theory made it the subject of intensive critical research centered in the twofold assumption of the identity of Dt with Josia's lawbook and the late date of its composition. The received Dt however is a work of many layers; which of them is the primitive form? Clearly, since Helcias refers to his discovery as a lawbook, at least the legislative chapters, 12–26, are meant. But the legislation too is heterogeneous, evincing both early and late elements. The primitive Dt is no creation from nothing; it demands further analysis of sources and accretions. Alternation between second person singular and second person plural is one basis on which critics have sought to separate the strands in Dt; their efforts however have been unproductive. The alternation does not occur throughout the entire book; it is moreover present in sections where there can be no question of a twofold source, as in the song of Moses, ch 32.

The Josian reforms resulting from the discovery give some clues to the contents of the book. The measures inaugurated by Josia are quite well covered by Dt 12–18; but one need not circumscribe the document by the king's action, for it could be that 4 Kgs 22–23 gives only a partial picture of the complete reform or that the renewal was principally concerned with cult.[17] Whatever the structure of Dt as it came to Josia the code in chs 12–26 best fits the description of the reforms, especially as regards the law of a single sanctuary.

In the critical struggle to confirm the identity and date of Josia's code there is no more fertile field of research than the legislation in Dt imposing worship in a single cultic center. The importance of the question is not limited to Dt but pertains even to the history of Hebrew cult and Yahwism. Some critics, holding that central worship was the custom from the beginning, refuse to admit that Dt introduces new legislation on a central sanctuary. The diatribes of the early prophets against the high places are used as evidence that Israel's tradition had always been central cult. The texts offered however seem directed more against what went on in the local sanctuary—idolatrous rites—than against the place itself; note for example Os 8:11: "When Ephraim made many altars to expiate sin, his altars became occasions of sin."

It is true that from ancient times certain great sanctuaries—Sichem, Silo, Bethel, Jerusalem—overshadowed local shrines and were places of special pilgrimage. Thus Elcana, husband of Anna, left his own city to sacrifice at Silo (1 Sm 1:3); and the establishment of the Ark of the Covenant in Jerusalem made that city the heart of cultic worship. Jeroboam I recognized the drawing power of Jerusalem when he set up rival centers at Dan and Bethel (3 Kgs 13:26–33). That there was a tendency to centralize the worship of Yahweh even in ancient times is quite possible; but to assert positively that the law and practice of centralized worship was a part of the Israelite tradition prior to Dt is to go beyond the evidence, especially in the light of texts clearly indicating a plurality of altars, such as 1 Sm 9:12; 14:35; 3 Kgs 18:30ff.

Later Judaism interpreted the Deuteronomic central sanctuary as Jerusalem. Significantly however Dt never refers to a specific shrine but only to the place "which the Lord, your God, chooses as the dwelling place for his name [*l⁰šakkēn š⁰mô*]," (Dt 12:11; 14:23). This "name theology" of the Deuteronomist is a refinement or corrective of earlier concepts of the manner of Yahweh's dwelling with Israel. According to Priestly traditions Yahweh in some manner abides within the Dwelling. One must specify "in some manner," for there is considerable variation among the traditions which speak of Yahweh's presence with his people. Although Yahweh directs: "They shall make a sanctuary for me, that I may dwell in their midst" (Ex 25:8; see also 29:45), most traditions agree that the Dwelling is not a permanent divine abode but the earthly spot to which Yahweh descended from time to time for the guidance of his people (see Ex 33:9; Nm 11:25; 12:5).

The early Priestly concept of Yahweh's dwelling with Israel was sublimated by the later interpretation that it was not Yahweh himself but his glory, the *k⁰bôd YHWH,* which entered the Dwelling in the form of a cloud. The earliest mention of this interpretation is a Priestly insertion in the Sinai narrative identifying the cloud covering Sinai with the glory of the Lord (Ex 24:16–17). Later at the completion of the Dwelling "the cloud covered the Meeting Tent and the glory of the Lord filled the Dwelling" (Ex 40:34; see also Lv 9:23).

The ancient concept of the place to which Yahweh descended gave way before the later traditions of the Sichemite amphictyony with its cult centered in the Ark. This is the tradition which came to dominate later Israelite history. Used as the

133

palladium of sacred warfare the Ark is almost identified with Yahweh himself: "Whenever the ark set out, Moses would say, 'Arise, O Lord, that your enemies may be scattered, and those who hate you may flee before you'" (Nm 10:35–36). The oft-repeated epithet "the Lord seated upon the cherubim" describes Yahweh, like a Semitic king, seated upon a throne supported by cherubim. This is the customary understanding of Yahweh's presence within the Holy of Holies in the Temple. The Ark as Yahweh's throne is a change from its purpose as a container for the commandments (Ex 25:16). In Ex 25:17–22 the ideas of chest and throne are combined: the gold propitiatory with its protective cherubim is mounted on the Ark containing the commandments; then from above the propitiatory Yahweh delivers his commands to Israel.

According to Deuteronomic traditions Yahweh and his glory do not dwell upon earth, neither in the Dwelling nor above the Ark, neither temporarily nor permanently. Instead Yahweh chooses a place for his name to dwell. The name is almost synonymous with the person of Yahweh; in a sense it is a kind of hypostasis. Given such a concept of Yahweh's dwelling with his people there could be for the Deuteronomist no question of the Ark as the throne of Yahweh; hence it became once again the cultic container for the commandments as in Dt 10:5: "After the Lord had given them to me, I turned and came down the mountain, and placed the tablets in the ark I had made. There they have remained, in keeping with the command the Lord gave me."

Although the Deuteronomic name theology is often regarded as a corrective for older and cruder representations of Yahweh's abiding with Israel, it should not be forgotten that the *kabôd* theology of the Priestly writer is already a sublimation of primitive concepts. And by reserving the word *šakan* (as contrasted with *yašab* elsewhere) to describe the divine dwelling on

134

earth, Priestly theology was attempting to resolve a certain tension between the notions of the immanence and transcendence of Yahweh. The blending and overlapping of traditions in both the D and P sources are one more indication of the antiquity of the materials involved. The motifs of the desert tent continued in later Israel; the Priestly tabernacle appears to be the climax of themes which began in the Mosaic tent.[18]

## The time and origins of Dt

Granted that Dt is Josia's lawbook, the year 621 gives only a terminal date for its composition, and the assumption that Dt is a contemporary work masquerading as an ancient writing is gratuitous. To critics in the first quarter of this century the determination of the time of the final redaction was no less intriguing than the pursuit of the primitive Dt. After veering back and forth between Mosaic and postexilic dates, scholars for the most part settled on an early seventh century date of composition. However the date of the final redaction is no longer considered so important as it once was, for modern critics have come to realize that even if Dt was not written until fairly late in Israel's history it nonetheless faithfully reflects the cherished traditions which had nourished Hebrew faith for centuries. Where in Israel did these traditions develop into Dt's highly individualistic presentation of the law? The attention given to the law of a single sanctuary first led to the opinion that the work was a mélange of the Jerusalem Temple rules reworked in the interests of centralization, broadened in social significance and fitted with an introduction reminiscent of the Elohist. But a large number of critics subscribes to the thesis that Dt embodies the preaching of the northern Levites whose traditions, formulated over several centuries, were brought into the southern kingdom after the fall of Samaria in 722.

The references to the amphictyonic Holy War, especially in chs 20, 21 and 24, suggest a military provenance readily explained by the political situation in the north. When the mercenaries of Israel fell to Assyria late in the eighth century the effort to build up home troops may well have revived the ideals of the ancient sacral amphictyony within a contemporary context of kingship and prophecy.[19] The spokesmen of the movement were the northern Levites. Not only did their position give them access to abundant sacral literature impregnated with theology but as Levites they also had close links with the Ark, the palladium of the Holy War in the tribal federation. Through their preaching they infused Mosaic traditions and laws with the renewed spirit of the old amphictyony and reiterated Israel's obligation of fervent response to Yahweh's election. What von Rad has called the Janus-like character of Dt, its fusion of the priestly and cultic with a national martial spirit, is explained by the northern origin of the work. Likewise Noth regards Dt as a revival of amphictyonic law; he believes that the ideal and seemingly impractical nature of some Deuteronomic legislation can be explained only if Dt is viewed as an effort to restore the basic tribal federation—for example the legislation on the sabbatical year in Dt 15:1–11. If Dt was conceived as a revival of amphictyonic law this would explain the presence of many ancient decrees, some of them certainly pre-Mosaic (Dt 14:3ff or 21:1ff).[20]

Generally speaking the determination of the primitive form of a law is no easier in Dt than in the other codes; yet the Deuteronomic legislation does afford clear instances of how earlier laws have been remodeled according to the redactor's ideology. A case in point is the amplification or reinterpretation of some ancient laws in terms of cultic centralization. The law of firstlings in Ex 13:12 for example reads: "You shall dedicate to the Lord every son that opens the womb; and all the male firstlings of your animals shall belong to the Lord." A similar law in Dt 15:19–20 adds: "Year after year you and your family shall eat them before the Lord, your God, in the place he chooses." The lawgiver even frankly admits the innovation: "You shall not do as we are now doing; here, everyone does what seems right to himself. . . . But . . . then to the place which the Lord, your God, chooses as the dwelling place for his name you shall bring all the offerings I command you" (Dt 12:8–10). Secondly, to make the law of centralization practical a distinction was made between profane and ritual slaughter of animals, a distinction never made in former times when all shedding of blood was regarded as somehow sacrificial. For similar practical reasons money could be substituted for the tithes brought to the cultic shrine (see for example Dt 14: 22–27).

## Content and style

Rewarding as investigations of chronology and development are, they have for too long a time detracted from the more pertinent and profitable exposition of the characteristics which give to Dt its power to engage the heart as well as the mind of the reader. In recent years the keen realization that biblical scholarship cannot live by criticism alone has occasioned new enthusiasm for biblical theology, albeit there is disagreement about the scope and methods—and even the definition—of such a discipline. But however defined, biblical theology cannot dispense with Dt, because here the message of salvation history as God revealing and man responding finds its most dramatic expression. Thus a more detailed examination of the contents and style of this book is in order.

Provided that the fundamental relation of law to the covenant is kept in mind, other legal corpora can be considered apart from the narratives into which they have been inserted; but the Deuteronomic legislation cannot be appreciated apart from the

137

framework of its prefatory and concluding chapters. Dt takes the form of three discourses of Moses, each with its own historical introduction, delivered in the plains of Moab during a period of forty days between the end of the desert wandering and the crossing of the Jordan. The three discourses begin at Dt 1:6, 5:1 and 27:1. Organization of disparate material around the figure of the great legislator imparts an impression of unity; a careful reading however discloses the composite nature of the material, especially in the introductory and concluding chapters. Material in the present framework defies efforts to impose order upon it. A brief summary of chs 1–11 will show the variety of independent elements, perhaps originally sermons, here amalgamated. The first chapter begins straightforwardly by announcing an address of Moses to all Israel as the people were about to cross the Jordan in the fortieth year of their wandering. The three chapters describing the background of Israel's present situation possess a kind of unity, although the sequence is not always clear. Having brought the people up to date, Moses declares: "Now, Israel, hear the statutes and decrees I am teaching you to observe" (Dt 4:1). But the recollection of the Sinai theophany and an exhortation to obedience delay the promised law. Ch 5 makes a fresh start: "Moses summoned all Israel and said to them, 'Hear, O Israel, the statutes and decrees . . .'" The legislation that follows is limited to the Decalogue and is thus incorporated into further remembrance of Sinai. Ch 6 takes up the necessity of obedience in the promised land; this leads in ch 7 to a discussion of how the pagans there are to be treated. Chs 9, 10 and 11 dwell upon imminent entrance into Palestine. Ch 12 at long last settles down to enumerating "the statutes and decrees which you must observe."

The framing chapters are linked to the law code by common vocabulary and style, both in the service of Deuteronomic ideology: obedience to Yahweh as a grateful response to his loving choice of Israel. Dt is not presentation of law as such but exhortation into which law has been inserted. It is difficult to escape the conclusion that Dt arose, in both the narrative and legislative sections, from the combination of sermons of different length. The preachers' message, ever the same, is reinforced not so much by a distinctive vocabulary (though typically Deuteronomic expressions occur) as by constant repetition of stock phrases. No remote deity has effected such wonders for Israel; it is "the Lord, your God" who has done all these things "with a strong hand and outstretched arm," leading her into the "land flowing with milk and honey."

Constantly the preacher reminds Israel of the love and fidelity which prompted Yahweh's deeds: "It was not because you are the largest of all nations that the Lord set his heart on you and chose you, for you are really the smallest of all nations. It was because the Lord loved you and because of his fidelity to the oath which he had sworn to your fathers, that he brought you out with his strong hand from the place of slavery" (Dt 7:7–8). "This day" Israel must answer the challenge of love; the only possible response is obedience to "the commands, the statutes, and the decrees," not as a legalistic condition for maintaining the covenant but as a grateful return for the mercies of the Lord. The use of set phrases conjures up a whole complex of ideas; "the Lord, your God" is a brief summation of the covenantal relationship; the "strong hand" and "great signs and wonders" recall the Exodus events; "this day" is a reminder that Yahweh is still effecting the covenant, still seeking his people's reply.

## Parenesis

The style of the Deuteronomic preaching is what one expects in a sermon: earnest exhortation—parenesis—and an appeal to the heart, a combination resulting in a certain redundance or even prolixity. When a law is proposed for observance the speaker comments upon it; he contrasts Israel's former behavior with what is now expected of her, details how the law is to be carried out and reminds his listeners of all the motives they have for its observance. The following passage shows the interplay of legislation and parenesis:

You shall not violate the rights of the alien or of the orphan, nor take the clothing of a widow as a pledge. For, remember, you were once slaves in Egypt, and the Lord, your God, ransomed you from there; that is why I command you to observe this rule.

When you reap the harvest in your field and overlook a sheaf there, you shall not go back to get it; let it be for the alien, the orphan or the widow, that the Lord, your God, may bless you in all your undertakings. When you knock down the fruit of your olive trees, you shall not go over the branches a second time; let what remains be for the alien, the orphan and the widow. When you pick your grapes, you shall not go over the vineyard a second time; let what remains be for the alien, the orphan and the widow. For remember that you were once slaves in Egypt; that is why I command you to observe this rule (Dt 24: 17–21).

Besides stirring Israel's memories by the use of phrases redolent of Yahweh's activity in her behalf the Deuteronomist often deliberately exhorts the people to remembrance. Remembering in the biblical sense is more than psychological recall; it brings the past into the present with compelling power. The verses just quoted contain the admonition to recall servitude in Egypt. Elsewhere the people are told to remember the days of old (Dt 32:7); the giving of the covenant (4:9–13); the sojourn in the desert (8:2; 9:7); even Yahweh (4:39–40; 6:6; 8:11). The juxtaposition of the "today" motif and the "remember" theme creates a remarkable contrast:

Be careful to observe all the commandments I enjoin on you today, that you may live and increase, and may enter in and possess the land which the Lord promised on oath to your fathers. Remember how for forty years now the Lord your God, has directed all your journeying in the desert, so as to test you by affliction and find out whether or not it was your intention to keep his commandments (8:1–2).

The two ideas form the point and counterpoint of Dt: on the one hand a recollection of Yahweh's deeds of yore; on the other the application of those deeds to Israel here and now.

## Purpose

All biblical laws, we have seen, are associated with the covenant; but the concept of the law as dynamic commitment to the alliance here and now—"this day"—is more accented in Dt than in any other legal corpus. Dt offers the strongest argument against the assumption that Israel viewed its relation to Yahweh as one based on law. Perhaps the argument comes through with such great force because the Deuteronomist is extremely conscious of the meaning of history in the religious sense, i.e. a vehement, single-minded renewal of the offer of salvation. No generation was perfectly faithful; renovation by a return to origins was always in order. In his own time the Deuteronomist sought to recoup Israel's losses, to save her religious patrimony by a return to the day the covenant was first established, a day which Yahweh mercifully repeats even for sinful Israel of a later age. Separated by centuries of complex and often tragic history, Israel at Sinai and the Deuteronomist's Israel at Horeb are still Yahweh's elect, and the word of the Lord is no less powerful "today" than in the "days of old."

After the Exile the work of the Deuteronomist came into its own and the great Deuteronomic theses forcibly penetrated Israelite thought. Some critics believe that predilection for Dt in the postexilic community occasioned a second redaction of the work. There is no doubt that Dt left its impress on the thought and writing of Israel; its spirit breathes in the later redactions of the historical books. Despite a growing tendency toward legalism the ideal of legal observance as a mark of fidelity to Yahweh and his covenant retained its hold upon Hebrew thought. When

141

Jesus asked the lawyer what the law had to say about gaining eternal life the lawyer answered readily in Deuteronomic terms of love for God and neighbor, not in terms of legal observance (Lk 10:25ff). The law that Jesus came to fulfill was law in the spirit of Dt, not the legal hairsplitting of some of his contemporaries. Early Christianity conceived law along the same lines as Dt: man's free response to God who in his love has chosen man.

## Conclusions

Israelite law, which stretches at intervals throughout the last four books of the Pentateuch, has been treated in the present chapter as a separate unit. This method was necessary in order to approach so vast a body of legislation with some degree of order, and to explain its origin and nature, its growth and modification and its role in Hebrew life. As much as possible however the codes should be kept in their proper context within the Pentateuch, lest they receive disproportionate emphasis by being removed from the rest of salvation history as recorded in the Pentateuch. The striking historical character of Hebrew religion led the sacred writers to imbed the legislative corpora within the narratives of the salvation history and it is within this framework that the narratives can best be understood. If salvation history is the story of God's proffer of salvation and man's response then law is a part of that history just as surely as are Yahweh's salvific acts, for law in its convenantal context assures man's total response. Law is communion with Yahweh through the adoption of his thoughts and ways.

# Footnotes to Chapter 2

[1] RSS (1962) 151.

[2] This is not to say that Priestly legislation is only a fabrication of a later age. Frank M. Cross, "The Tabernacle," BA 10 (1947) 52, notes: "While the Priestly account is schematized and idealized, and while the Priestly writers read the theological interpretations and historical development of later ages into their system, nevertheless, Priestly traditions must be deemed an important historical witness to the Mosaic age." Cross's article is also printed in *The Biblical Archaeologist Reader,* ed G. Ernest Wright and David Noel Freedman, 201–28.

[3] ANET (Princeton 1950) 163, 176. The principal codes are translated in this volume, 159–98.

[4] Ibid, 165.

[5] *Die Ursprünge des israelitischen Rechts* contains Alt's fullest treatment of casuistic and apodictic law. The work is reprinted in his *Kleine Schriften zur Geschichte des Volkes Israel* (Munich 1953) I, 278–332.

[6] Theophile Meek however asserts that apodictic law occurs also in extra-biblical codes; see his translation of the Middle Assyrian laws, ANET, 183, n24. De Vaux, op cit 147, suggests that Hittite treaties may offer parallels to Hebrew apodictic law.

[7] Many Hittite treaties are extant; see ANET, 201–03, for the text of the treaty between Hattusilis and Rameses II. For a fuller treatment of both law and covenant in Israel see George E. Mendenhall, "Ancient Oriental and Biblical Law," BA 17 (1954) 26–46, and "Covenant Forms in Israelite Tradition," BA 17 (1954) 50–76.

[8] *Das formgeschichtliche Problem* in *Gesammelte Studien,* 33–35. James Muilenburg, "Form and Structure of the Covenantal Formulations," VT 9 (1959) 347–65, views the covenant as a literary form. He centers his analysis in Ex 19:3–6, which he regards as a royal proclamation resembling treaties or epilogues to law corpora. The form contains three elements: calling Israel to witness Yahweh's great deeds, exhortation to commitment and enumeration of the benefits of this commitment. Muilenburg lists similar pericopes throughout the Pentateuch (355).

[9] See for example his *The History of Israel,* tr by P. R. Ackroyd, 2d rev ed (New York 1960) 53–138.

[10] Rudolf Otto's *The Idea of the Holy: An Inquiry into the Non-rational Factor in the Idea of the Divine and Its Relation to the Rational,* tr John

W. Harvey (Oxford 1923) is an important study of the notion of holiness as found in all religions, but it does not always acknowledge the unique features of Yahwism.

[11] Obedience to the law was also demanded by the prophets. Too much has been made of the opposition between the law and the prophets, as if this indicated some fundamental disagreement about the nature of religion. H. H. Rowley, "The Unity of the Old Testament," BJRylL 29 (1946) 326–58, shows that the prophetic "rejection" of law and cult has been greatly exaggerated.

[12] Walther Eichrodt, *Theology of the Old Testament,* tr J. A. Baker (London 1961) I, 51–63, treats the supposed neglect of the covenant by the classic prophets. For the impact of the law during and after the Exile see Salo W. Baron, *A Social and Religious History of the Jews,* 8 vol, 2d ed (Philadelphia 1951–56) I, *passim* and 140–48.

[13] "Book of the Covenant" is commonly interpreted as referring to Ex 20:22—23:19, but this is sometimes disputed. Ex 34:28 seems to identify the Book of the Covenant with the Ten Commandments: "Moses . . . wrote on the tablets the words of the covenant, the Ten Commandments." However the proximity of Ex 34:28 to the Ritual Decalogue in Ex 34:14–26 has led some critics to identify the Book of the Covenant with the Ritual Decalogue; see Robert Pfeiffer, "The Oldest Decalogue," JBL 43 (1924) 294–310. Doubtless the law collections have been shifted from their original positions, and it is impossible to assign all references correctly. Moreover the entire Sinai pericope is very involved and the separation of its components is extremely difficult.

[14] Rowley, "Moses and the Decalogue," BJRylL 34 (1951) 116, states: "The familiar Ten Commandments cannot be considered without relation to the Ritual Decalogue of Exod. XXXIV." He holds that the ritual decrees are somewhat older, being the primitive form circulated among the Kenites. Moses developed the ethical Decalogue not from the earlier cultic corpus, but from a still more ancient source which at some time forked into two streams of development, cultic and ethical.

[15] Darkness shrouds the origin and primitive significance of the major Hebrew feasts. Passover may have been celebrated in Egypt; other feasts were doubtless borrowed from Canaan. By the time they appear in the oldest Ex accounts, the celebrations had already taken on new meaning and imply a sedentary people whose agricultural concerns are echoed in the feasts.

The feast of Pentecost, originally marking the start of the barley harvest, soon took on religious significance by association with the giving of the law on Sinai. The complete identification of the Passover with the Exodus is a product of late theologizing. It is noteworthy that the Priestly legislation in the Holiness Code (Lv 23:5) does not mention Exodus in connection with the feast of Passover, even though the narrative describing the Exodus and original Passover (Ex 12:1—13:2) and the second Passover (Nm 9:1–14) are from the pen of the Priestly writer. For a full general treatment of the ancient Hebrew feasts see de Vaux, op cit, 484–506.

[16] See Norbert Lohfink, "Die Bundesurkunde des Königs Josias," Bib 44

(1963) 261–288. Lohfink asserts that the document was a "book of the covenant," not Dt.

17 Josia's reform is compiex and difficult to interpret. Comparison of the accounts in 4 Kgs 22–23 and 2 Chr 35 allows the possibility that Josia's reform was in progress before 621. The sole features prompted by the discovery of the book may have been covenant renewal and the celebration of the Passover in a central sanctuary.

18 For further discussion see Gerhard von Rad's "Deuteronomy's 'Name Theology' and the Priestly Document's 'Kabôd Theology,'" *Studies in Deuteronomy*, tr David Stalker (Chicago 1953) 37–44; and Cross's "The Priestly Tabernacle," 45–68.

19 Kingship however receives little emphasis. The Davidic monarchy and messianism, natural ideas in Juda, are neglected. Here is further indication that Dt originated in sections where the sacral notions of kingship had not taken such deep root, i.e. in the north, perhaps in Sichem, headquarters of the amphictyony; see von Rad, *Studies in Deuteronomy*, 60–62.

20 Martin Noth, *Die Gesetze im Pentateuch* (Halle 1940) 28, 34–40.

# 3

## Pentateuchal Studies since Wellhausen

A description of the slow growth of the Pentateuch and the various hypotheses about its origins is not to our interest or purpose here. Summaries of the theories leading up to the classic exposition by Julius Wellhausen have been made often enough.[1] Our concern rather is with the development Wellhausen's theory underwent at the hands of his colleagues, both Catholic and non-Catholic. Consequently it will suffice to give only a brief summary of classic Wellhausenism as a point of departure for our discussion of subsequent progress in Pentateuchal studies.

### Wellhausenism

A century and a quarter before Wellhausen, Jean d'Astruc observed that variation in the divine names in Gn indicates two memoirs. In 1780 J. S. Eichhorn analyzed the Pentateuch through Lv, confirmed the presence of two records and gave them the sigla J and E. Near the turn of the century Karl Ilgen scrutinized the E narrative more closely and divided it into two strands: $E^1$ (later P) and $E^2$ (later E). Martin de Wette in 1805 completed the list by his separation of source D.

It is well known of course that J represents the Yahwist

146

writer; E the Elohist; D the Deuteronomist; and P the Priestly writer. J and E were originally distinguished by their use of the divine name Yahweh and Elohim respectively, but the variations between them go much deeper than this single contrast. Some confusion obtains in understanding the sigla used by earlier critics. It is not always clear whether E refers to the work of the Priestly writer and to that of the present Elohist (this was Eichhorn's usage) or to the Elohist alone (the $E^2$ of Ilgen). The sources were originally called J and E; these subsequently became J, $E^1$ and $E^2$; and finally J, P and E.

The distinction made of the four principal documents, plus many lesser ones, was greeted in some quarters with misgivings. It was asked whether, in the interest of the unity of the books, it would not be more prudent to posit a basic document and regard the other "documents" as interpolations and complements. Some critics resorted to a theory of fragments, thus destroying the unity of the books. But in 1853 Hermann Hupfeld's convincing restatement of the documentary theory won over most of the supporters of the theory of complements or of fragments.

The absolute date of the strata was customarily regarded as the time of Moses, and their relative chronology was indicated by the sequence P, E, J, D. Then de Wette's assertion that Dt was the lawbook found in the Temple (4 Kgs 22:8–13) and attributed —as a pious fraud—to the great Moses created new interest in the dating. If Dt was composed only shortly before its discovery in 621 then the whole tradition of Mosaic authorship of the Pentateuch was suspect. More evidence of late composition accrued. In 1869 Karl Graf, following his teacher Eduard Reuss, and profiting by the criticism of Abraham Kuenen, climaxed his Pentateuchal studies by positing a postexilic date for the composition of both the legislative and narrative sections.

Out of these disparate elements of the documentary theories evolving in the nineteenth century Julius Wellhausen made a forceful and definitive synthesis. A series of articles in 1876 and 1877 indicated the general features of his system, but it was his *Prolegomena zur Geschichte Israels* of 1883 which assured the triumph of his views. Since the main outlines of his thesis do not differ radically from those of his immediate predecessors, Wellhausen's success can be attributed at least in part to his presentation, remarkable for its forceful reasoning and conviction. Wellhausen's early interest and training in history left their mark upon his theory, for he mounted literary conclusions within the framework of Israelite religious history. His historical concepts in turn depended upon the Hegelian doctrines of immanence and synthesis, which Wellhausen employed in explaining the evolution of Israelite religion and culture.[2]

Wellhausen worked with the Hexateuch, i.e. the five books of Moses and Jos, combined on the grounds of identical literary characteristics and subject matter. The term became current in nineteenth century biblical studies but had been used long before by Bonfrère (1625), Spinoza (1670) and Geddes (1792). In recent years however some critics (principally Martin Noth and the Scandinavian school) prefer to speak of the Tetrateuch, i.e. the first four books of Moses. They argue that since D, found only rarely in the first four books, continues into the historical books where J, E and P are not found, Dt should be separated from the Pentateuch and placed at the head of the so-called Deuteronomic history, which extends from Jos to Kgs inclusive. Wellhausen posited within the Hexateuch four main documents: J, E, D and P, in that order of relative chronology. First there are the narrative sections of J and E, dating from around 870 and 770 respectively. The redaction of these texts occurred around 680, followed by the writing of Dt (at least the core chapters, 12–26) and other D elements shortly before their discovery in 621. The composition of P began only with the Exile, perhaps under Ezechiel, and continued until the final re-

148

daction of the Hexateuch during the reforms of Ezra and Nehemia in the second half of the fifth century. The assignment of late dates to the documents and to their redaction not only precluded Mosaic authorship but also interchanged the dates commonly ascribed to the prophets and the Hexateuch. This reversal, a pivotal point in Wellhausen's system, occasioned repercussions in all fields of Old Testament study.

Basic to the classic documentary theory were certain presuppositions shared in common with nineteenth century scholarship. First, there was a general skepticism regarding history. Using newly formulated scientific concepts, critics were loath to concede historicity to accounts of noncontemporaneous events. Second, because of the pervasive effects of Hegelianism, some scholars assumed that the culture and religion of ancient peoples had evolved gradually from earlier primitive forms. Thus ethical monotheism was considered the climax of a slow advance from manistic and animistic beliefs. A similar development could be traced in the evolution of agricultural life from nomadism. There was finally an apriori rejection of all supernatural elements in the history of Israel. Although Yahwism was acknowledged as a unique phenomenon it required no supernatural explanation; it could be accounted for by the same principle of immanence responsible for the cultural and religious growth of other ancient peoples. The presuppositions bore the seeds of future disillusionment; the inadequacies of the hypothesis, realized only slowly, can be laid at the door of this apriorism.

There were moreover other weaknesses which would appear in time. The assumption of Israel's isolation from her neighbors determined the historical pattern into which Wellhausen fitted his documentary theory; when the pattern was demonstrated to be erroneous the classic hypothesis associated with it was also shaken. The findings of archeology began to establish the close cultural relations between all the peoples of the Near East, and the vast treasures of ancient literature revealed extrabiblical parallels for many Israelite institutions and laws.

Yet such deficiencies, scarcely evident at first, did not hamper the ever wider and ever more enthusiastic acceptance of the documentary theory. Because of Wellhausen's consistent and cogent exposition, Hexateuchal studies dominated biblical criticism. The thesis greatly influenced the study of the rest of the Old Testament as well, for scholars extended the documents beyond the Hexateuch into Jgs, Sm and Kgs, even allying them with the prophets Jeremia and Ezechiel. In addition the assignment of the prophetic writings to a time prior to the composition of the Hexateuch radically altered the concept of the prophets' mission: they became the originators of monotheism, not its renovators. This notion of the prophetic role had a profound impact on the study and interpretation of the prophetic writings.

The extension and triumph of Wellhausen's system did not go unchallenged. To Catholics and non-Catholics alike the assertions that dogmatic supernaturalism is untenable and that critical canons must be totally independent of theology brought genuine pain, the more so since reconciliation of faith and fact seemed impossible. Of all the objectionable features of Wellhausenism its rationalistic, apriori rejection of the supernatural loomed largest; it overshadowed all else and caused the theory to be condemned totally. Then, as the inadequacies of the four source theory became more apparent, even critics who entertained no objections on dogmatic grounds began to doubt whether the methods of literary analysis proposed by Wellhausenism were really an aid in achieving the goal of exegesis: the full understanding of a writer and his work. Some enthusiastic proponents of the documentary theory embarked on careers of further analysis, producing critical extravaganzas which split and resplit the sources until the books were atomized.[3] The barrenness of such investigations caused many critics to wonder whether, now that the verses had been subjected to literary scrutiny and neatly parceled out among J, E, P and D, there was anything left to be said.

## Hermann Gunkel and *Gattungsforschung*

Among reactions to the documentary theory the *Gattungsforschung* of Hermann Gunkel was the most successful,[4] but its opposition to Wellhausenism should not be exaggerated. Gunkel believed in fact that the establishment of documents was an essential of biblical research; and only because he considered this work successfully accomplished did he assume the tasks proposed in his new method. With literary criticism as such he had no quarrel. No one can deny the necessity, the indispensability of literary criticism. Nevertheless he deplored the fact that literary method in practice confined itself to a critique of the state and origin of the sources, or to the minute philological analyses in the sources. Such an approach to the Bible presupposes that one is dealing, literally, with scripture—i.e. matter transmitted in written documents. Gunkel contended that the variations in the Pentateuch are to be accounted for not by ascribing J, E, D and P to various authors as free compositions, but by recognizing separate preliterary and even oral traditions from which the written documents eventually developed. To achieve its proper goal exegesis must go beyond literary analysis and provide a history of Israelite literature.

Gunkel had no illusions that a history could be written establishing the genesis of a work in chronological sequence. Rather he affirmed our ignorance of the date and authorship of almost the entire Old Testament. With the written sources as his starting point the historian of Israelite literature must,

151

Gunkel felt, separate the units of tradition from their secondary context in the documents and penetrate to the original data which are their foundation. In this process of course the author cannot be completely disregarded; still it must be noted that the Israelite religion, conservative in form and content, is more interested in the typical than in the individual and expresses this interest in definite, conventional categories or *Gattungen;* thus the historian's first task is to determine the form in which the thought is clothed. A knowledge of the particular situation giving rise to the form—the *Sitz im Leben* or life setting—is therefore indispensable. Whoever wants to understand the form must clarify its situation and ask: "Who is the speaker; who are the hearers?" On the basis of stylistic elements, content and interest the detached original unit is defined: e.g. etiological legend, taunt song or dirge.

In the determination of literary form Gunkel's method was especially interested in myth, already a preoccupation of historians of religion. After denying historicity to biblical accounts, critics found it an easy matter, especially if they were devotees of comparative religion, to find myth everywhere. Gunkel denied however that true myth is contained in the Bible. Although mythic elements abound in the legends he insisted that Israelite monotheism rendered them colorless and eliminated all their grosser aspects. (It might be noted that recent criticism questions a definition which considers myth necessarily polytheistic and suggests that myth relates more to the manner of thought than to the content.[5]) Once isolated and placed in its life setting the original datum must be followed as it develops, becomes a part of large cycles and then changes into the entity found in the present Scripture. It does not suffice to analyze a book or a passage down to its smallest primitive components. This preliminary work should lead the critic to collate his observations by constructing a history of the literary forms. Gunkel himself

152

appeared to be less successful in writing such a history than in describing and defining the forms.

Tracing this development is a delicate and tedious process. Invaluable assists in this study are recent archeological discoveries and the newly found literatures of the ancient Near East. Striking extrabiblical parallels to Israelite life and literature have been increasingly utilized for the investigation of Hebrew genres and life settings, though perhaps not always with due recognition of the changes Israel made of borrowed materials. Form criticism works necessarily with small blocks of tradition, but the total effect of the complexes must be kept in mind if the resulting "book" is to be understood. The achievement of the undertaking is arduous, and Gunkel is careful to note the demands it makes of the critic. True exegesis is more than a word-by-word, sentence-by-sentence explanation. The living soul of the writer, the totality of his experience, the complexity of his entire being—these are the subjects of exegesis. The critic must mirror the ancient writer purely and clearly, for the critic is not the master of his material but the servant. Because of his attention to the esthetic and creative aspects of criticism Gunkel has often been called "a scientific Herder." But for Gunkel the esthetic considerations are always secondary: the exegete is a theologian, not an esthetician.

It is hardly an exaggeration to say that Gunkel's method has directed the whole course of twentieth century biblical criticism. By its emphasis on oral tradition and by the use of archeological and literary materials of the ancient Near East, it has approached nearer the living reality which produced the tradition and thus has supplied for the weaknesses of a static documentary criticism. Nevertheless form criticism is not without some difficulties of its own. For example Gunkel contends, and with reason, that the earliest traditions were oral. Since oral delivery necessarily requires that the transmitted material be compact, he makes

153

brevity the criterion of age and asserts, mistakenly, that the shortest accounts are necessarily the most primitive. Always of the purest style, these ancient forms lose vigor and distinction as they develop. Here, for Gunkel, is the tragedy of Israelite literature: the spirit departs; servile imitation appears; and labored editing replaces creative genius. Further, consonant with his view that a chronological literary history of Israel is impossible, Gunkel proposed that objective elements of history, though not irrelevant, are not to be found in biblical writings.

Finally, though not in itself irreligious or antireligious, form criticism lends itself perhaps more readily to evolutionistic, naturalistic tendencies in certain of its practitioners.

### Gunkel's followers

The rapprochement with Wellhausen has been continued by Gunkel's followers but their views on the documents present no solid front. As Gunkel's foremost collaborator, Hugo Gressmann indefatigably explored the influence of the peoples of the Near East on Israel, particularly in religion, for his chief interest was history of religion. In studying the development of Israel he stressed mythic elements more than Gunkel did, holding that they had preserved intact their primitive value.

Johannes Hempel was the first to attempt a history of Hebrew literature according to Gunkel's dictum that the history of Israelite literature is the history of its literary forms. The investigation of the small primitive units exemplified in Hebrew law was Albrecht Alt's forte. His research contributed to an understanding of biblical legislation and provided the classic distinction between apodictic and casuistic law. Martin Noth sets for himself the task of reconstructing the history of the traditions by isolating themes and by pushing back to the initial stages of the tradition. To Gerhard von Rad it is as important to know the

154

resultant whole as it is to differentiate the contributing sources. The critic must examine not the primitive tradition alone but also its new import in the final composition, for the inner significance of a tradition is altered when built into comprehensive themes of a greater whole.

Different from one another though they are, these compatriots of Gunkel employed the methodology of form criticism as envisaged by its founder. In the hands of its Scandinavian practitioners however form criticism underwent a few radical changes. The northern critics, by increasing the emphasis on oral tradition and by concentrating on the cultic aspects of myth, so altered Gunkel's system as to form a separate school—even though the aims and methods of this school are still not generally agreed upon. Johannes Pedersen first indicated the direction the Scandinavian critics were taking when he rejected the documentary theory and broadened the concept of the sociological factors of the life setting. Sigmund Mowinckel, one of Gunkel's most brilliant students and a distinguished literary critic as well, went far beyond his master in the analysis of cultic and ritual aspects of myth and thus established one of the dominant interests of the Scandinavian school.

A further break with the documentary thesis came with H. S. Nyberg's assertion of the primacy of oral tradition. These traditions, says Nyberg, are not rigid. They suffer change and deterioration but they nonetheless furnish the critic with living material, not with dead texts. This emphasis on dynamic oral tradition focuses critical analysis on the recovery of the original elements of the tradition, e.g. the very words of the prophets. Still more radical was Ivan Engnell who in 1945 declared the complete inadequacy of literary criticism and even of form criticism insofar as either admits of written sources or redactions. To be valid, Engnell asserts, criticism must work solely with blocks of oral tradition; these blocks furthermore are always of cultic

155

origin. His traditio–historical method seeks to penetrate to the primitive datum and to delineate its development—quite literally a history of the tradition. Through his attention to oral tradition and to cult Sigmund Mowinckel has had great influence upon the school of Uppsala, but he differs sharply from the group in regard to stability of oral transmission and the exclusive validity of the traditio-historical method. In fact Mowinckel has gone so far as to charge that no formulation in principle of what this method means or should mean has yet appeared.

The chief features of the school of Uppsala—the primacy of oral tradition and cult—are also its principal weaknesses. Oral tradition, especially as regards its stability, can scarcely support the demands the Scandinavians make of it. Furthermore if spoken material is so reliable then it constitutes a source resembling the Wellhausen documents spurned by Uppsala. The Scandinavians' description of Israelite cult, based on analogies with cults of neighboring peoples, sometimes presumes institutions and observances for which there is no cogent proof. At other times the Uppsala school neglects the peculiar use Israel made of borrowed materials.

## The present state of Pentateuchal studies

What is the present state of Pentateuchal criticism? Recent biblical study outside Scandinavia generally presupposes documents, but in its concept of sources scholarship has moved a long way from the original hypothesis of J, E, D and P as the writings of individual authors. With a flexible documentary theory for its basis, contemporary criticism now uses the methodology of form criticism to achieve a truer and richer understanding of biblical thought by searching out its origin and development. The practice of contemporary critics bears out the contention that Old Testament research can be neither exclusively literary criticism nor exclusively an analysis of oral traditions; it must combine in its methodology both literary and form investigations. That the newer methods have not dispensed with the classic system is evident in the persevering influence of the four-source theory. Regardless of the changes Wellhausenism has undergone at the hands of both supporters and opponents, the most telling witness to its value is the fact that in the seventy years since its formulation no hypothesis commanding broad assent has been advanced to replace it. Pure Wellhausenism is now only an historical phenomenon; but the rudiments of J, E, D and P and the characteristics of these four strata are still in possession; no biblical critic can afford to ignore them.

## Catholic reaction to Wellhausenism

In contrast to the confident and, in some cases, brilliant advances in non-Catholic criticism, Catholic biblical scholarship of the nineteenth century had heavy going at best. Exegetes had paid little heed to the documentary theory in its initial stages; their interests were elsewhere. Because rapidly progressing physical sciences had arrogantly summoned the Bible to the bar of judgment, Catholic exegetes labored to make the sacred writings scientifically acceptable. Materialistic science endangered the doctrines of inerrancy and inspiration of Scripture. The development of an adequate theory of inspiration therefore became a prime concern of Catholic exegetes. But valuable as their effort was it had little effect on rationalistic higher criticism, which regards revelation, the supernatural and inspiration as irrelevant. When the documentary theory, with the momentum of a century of evolution behind it, appeared in the compelling exposition of Julius Wellhausen, Catholics began to realize that more was at stake than a plausible explanation of the days of creation. As Wellhausenism continued to sweep critical defenses before it,

Catholics in general, shocked at the coolness with which the theory demolished the supernatural, flatly rejected the system. Every concession was branded compromise; no attempt was made to distinguish methods and conclusions from the underlying rationalistic philosophy. Counterattacks simply reiterated traditional positions.

## Marie-Joseph Lagrange

Not all Catholic critics however chose to remain in a state of siege. One of the first attempts to meet the documentary theory on its own grounds was made during the Catholic scientific congress held in Fribourg, Switzerland in 1897, when Marie-Joseph Lagrange O.P. (1855–1938) appealed courageously and realistically for a positive response to the challenge of higher criticism.[6] To clear the ground for such a reply he examined five "questions préjudicielles" to determine whether the objections to the investigation of Pentateuchal sources were legitimate and cogent.

First Lagrange considered the question of redaction. How, if Mosaic authorship is to be sustained, can editing subsequent to Moses be conceded? The difficulty disappears, says Lagrange, if we drop the modern western concept of authorship and return to that of the ancient orientals. In their eyes an author's rights were not inviolable. A book is quite impersonal; one may add to it or rearrange it without denying attribution to the original author. Granted then that redaction is compatible with a Mosaic authorship, will not the admission of evolution in the legislation be a concession to Wellhausenism? Hardly, for every good law considers the needs of subjects, and the needs—and therefore the laws—change according to circumstances. Lagrange points out that the Jerusalem priests had the power to promulgate laws in the name of God. If their measures conformed to primitive law

158

then their legislation was considered Mosaic. Hence the formula "God said to Moses" declares that the law is both divine and Mosaic; it is tantamount to saying: "Here is a law emanating from divine authority according to the mind of the first law-giver."

But it would also seem that scriptural testimony to Mosaic authorship is so definite as to preclude any discussion of individual documents. Lagrange is well aware of the battery of texts assembled to sustain Moses' role as writer of the Pentateuch, but points out that in none of these texts is there contained a categorical, formal declaration of Mosaic authorship. Critics persist with a fourth, similar objection: what of the testimony of tradition paralleling that of Scripture? The patristic tradition of Mosaic authorship is freely granted—but what significance is to be attached to it? Lagrange contends that where a tradition does not involve a matter of faith, even the unanimous consent of the Fathers does not render it certain. And here Lagrange distinguishes a twofold tradition: literary and historical; his classic distinction has been widely accepted by those who uphold substantial Mosaic authorship. Granted that both traditions are valid, the literary tradition is not so cogent as the historical. The literary tradition represents a double current: that of the Jews, who trace the Pentateuch back to Sinai; and that of the Fathers, who refer to the Pentateuch as the work of Ezra. In time the Jewish view prevailed, but the existence of the other tradition shows that the matter was not always so firmly fixed as it now appears to be.

The fifth and last question is the historicity of the books of Moses. The postulation of additions and redactions after Moses seems to threaten the veracity and historicity of the entire Pentateuch. But is the recital of events occurring centuries earlier necessarily a tissue of myth? If so, says Lagrange, then Moses deceived his people about events in patriarchal times. If Moses used sources for this early history then why deny a similar privilege to those who followed him? Furthermore, according to Lagrange, in any query concerning the historicity of biblical texts the exegete must disavow modern European ideas and accept historical concepts as they were conceived by the Semites. The recitation of objective historical details is not the concern of salvation history. Where historical reality is lacking, Lagrange asks whether it is not because of the genre the biblical writer has employed.

## *Lagrange:* La méthode historique

Five years after the Fribourg congress Lagrange in *La méthode historique*[7] entered a plea for biblical criticism practiced according to sound historical method and demonstrated the application of such procedure to a number of the besetting problems of exegesis: the relation of criticism to dogma, to science and to history. Against those who feared that the use of the historical method is not consonant with the first duty of the Catholic critic—submission to the authority of the Church—Lagrange affirmed the possibility of combining scientific criticism with the respect due to defined dogma. His principle sounds fair enough in the abstract; can it be reduced to practice? How for example can the exegete, while upholding the immutability of truth, explain the development of dogma, especially in the Old Testament? The evolutionist theory of culture and religion finds little favor with Catholics; yet its rejection should not blind them to the growth of doctrine apparent in the Bible. In tracing this growth, Lagrange insists, it is essential to introduce the historical method into the study of Scripture, just as the middle ages united philosophy and faith in the study of theology.[8]

A second critical problem, of special concern to students of the Pentateuch, is the relation of science to the biblical narra-

160

tives; here Lagrange reiterates the teaching that the Bible offers no scientific instruction. He castigates the eager desire to bring Scripture into agreement with science, and the opposite, equally insidious error of making science bear witness to faith. The extent to which the Bible contains science has already been expounded in Leo XIII's *Providentissimus Deus* but Catholic exegesis, still somewhat nervous before the self-assured, patronizing airs of progressive science, was eager to vindicate biblical cosmology. Lagrange notes wryly that it is because of its excessive regard for science that Catholic exegesis has lumbered so heavily through the first chapter of Gn. When treating the scriptural narratives, Lagrange says, exegesis should not ask whether history is contained therein. This he grants. Rather his question is whether anything besides history is contained therein. According to the view of Catholic and many other scholars, primitive history, beginning with the origin of man, was handed down to Abraham. Anthropological evidence confirming the great antiquity of the human race contradicts this view, for the long transmission of primitive history without writing and without a magisterium is inexplicable. Regarding those portions of the Bible having the appearance of history therefore the first task in determining their value is to analyze their literary genres. Only thus can the true character of the narratives be estimated.

## The Church and Pentateuchal studies

### Modernism and biblical studies

Had the course charted by Lagrange been followed the story of Catholic Pentateuchal studies in the early twentieth century would have been far different. Unfortunately however the rise of modernism necessitated precautions which halted this promis-

161

ing beginning and restrained biblical criticism within narrowly defined limits. Modernism was an amorphous growth, rendered more treacherous by its facile combination of truth and error, as well as by its insidious attack on dogmas at their very roots. The Church throughout the centuries has faced the necessity of preaching the good news in terms suited to the mentality and spirit of each particular age. This process of adaptation constantly runs the risk of compromising the gospel in order to adapt it to a changed intellectual outlook. Such a danger was particularly acute in the late nineteenth century when the spirit of rationalistic criticism permeated theological studies, demanding that Christianity reassess its origins and purpose in the light of scientific advances. In European university circles many scholars whose efforts were originally devoted to an explication of Catholic positions presently adopted positions untenable by Catholic orthodoxy. Their deviation was not so much an attack on a body of determined doctrine as the assumption of vaguely defined heretical attitudes prompting their theological speculations. So numerous were its ramifications in all fields of Catholic thought that the exposition and condemnation of its errors required one of the lengthiest encyclicals of all times: Pius X's *Pascendi.* Emphasizing the chameleon-like character of the modernist, the pontiff noted that the man of this persuasion sustained within himself a manifold personality: he was simultaneously a philosopher, a theologian, an historian, an apologist and a reformer.

The leading traits of the heresy—the use of Hegelian immanentism and nineteenth century historicism—exerted such influence in the field of Scripture studies that Pius X could say of modernist scholars: "When they write history they make no mention of the divinity of Christ, but when they are in the pulpit they profess it clearly. . . . In the same way they draw their distinctions between exegesis which is pastoral and theological and exegesis which is scientific and historical."[9] The most prominent of the modernists was Alfred Loisy, an exegete and orientalist

162

teaching at the Institut Catholique in Paris. His shrewd and penetrating critical writings made him the center of bitter controversy from about 1890 onward; the distrust he aroused in orthodox circles was often transferred to Catholic exegetes in general. Loisy's sharp distinction between the Christ of faith and the Christ of history led him to an implicit denial of the transcendent and the supernatural in the origins of Christianity. It is not surprising that in drawing up her battlelines against modernism the Church evinced cautious reserve toward any biblical criticism which jeopardized traditional positions. Of the sixty-five propositions in the decree *Lamentabili,* which preceded the 1907 encyclical by a few months, nineteen deal directly or indirectly with Scripture. A summary of those propositions concerning the Old Testament will reveal the dangers of modernism to the true study and interpretation of the sacred writings.

The modernist asserts first of all that God is not the author of Scripture. Inspiration, which does not extend to all parts of the Bible, simply means that the Hebrew writers handed down religious doctrine in a manner not well understood by gentiles. The exegete must therefore free himself from all preconceived notions of supernaturality and interpret the Bible as a human document. The Church's elucidation of Scripture must be corrected by the more accurate judgment of exegetes, for the teachings of the Church cannot be reconciled with the true account of the origin of Christianity. Especially where scientific matters are involved the Church has no right to judge. Even dogmatic definitions by the Church cannot determine the proper sense of Scripture; hence condemnations by the Roman congregations are of little moment.

## 1906 decrees of the Pontifical Biblical Commission

Catholic studies suffered a still sharper curtailment in the 1906 decrees of the Pontifical Biblical Commission on Mosaic author-

163

ship of the Pentateuch. Selecting the question of Mosaic authorship as the heart of the Pentateuchal problems consequent upon
higher criticism, the Commission in four succinct decrees set the
course of Catholic biblical scholarship for the next forty years.[10]
The cautious wording of the document is the result not of the
Commission's unwillingness to commit itself, but of its respect
for both Catholic tradition and the demands of scientific scholarship. Without excluding new conclusions warranted by evidence,
the decisions discourage rash acceptance of the results of higher
criticism. The first decree for example does not reject outright
the arguments garnered by critics against Mosaic authorship, but
it does deny that such arguments give the right to affirm—"ius
tribuant affirmandi"—that Moses did not write the Pentateuch.

Having thus affirmed but not defined Mosaic authorship, the
decrees consider the sources prior to Moses and the additions
and the modifications posterior to him. In the second statement
the meaning of authorship is discussed—cautiously and nega-
tively. Actual writing or dictation by Moses is not demanded; it
is possible that the composition, conceived by Moses under divine
inspiration, was commissioned to others who faithfully repro-
duced his thoughts. The nature of Moses' supervision and influence, so pervasive as to justify the attribution of authorship, is
not discussed. The difficulties the Mosaic authorship suggests
are analogous to those presented by the joint authorship of God
and the sacred writer of the inspired books of the Bible.

The first two pronouncements of the Commission suggest that
the work done by "some other person or persons" was contemporaneous with that of Moses. The third decree however introduces the question of sources, whether written documents or
oral traditions, that are anterior to Moses. The Commission declares that no prejudice to Mosaic authorship is entailed in the
use of such sources. These materials, according to the Commission, whether oral or written, were used with great selectivity

164

and summarized or amplified according to need—but always under the influence of inspiration.

By its use of "substantially" ("salva substantialiter mosaica authentia et integritate Pentateuchi")—essentially a qualitative, not a quantitative term—the last decree helps to define the nature of the authorship that is to be assigned to Moses. It also notes that the centuries after Moses' death brought modifications and additions of various sorts: appendages by an inspired author, substitution of new words and forms for old, glosses and explanations. The investigation of these accretions and mutations according to the laws of sound criticism is the legitimate work of the Catholic exegete.

To sum up, the Commission offered four directives to students of the Bible: first, the findings of higher criticism, weighty though they may be, are not sufficient to permit the denial of Mosaic authorship; second, the claim that Moses wrote the Pentateuch does not necessarily postulate actual writing or dictation by him. Third, the use of documents or oral traditions, either literally or in substance, does not prejudice Mosaic authenticity; finally, while affirming substantial Mosaic authorship, one can freely admit that changes were later made in the Pentateuch, and it is the province of the critic to investigate these changes.

On examination the decrees are less precise than they may at first appear. The pronouncements concern Moses as the writer of the Pentateuch; yet nowhere is the word "author" defined, and the limits of "substantialiter" are undetermined. The secretaries allowed in the second decree really solve no problem. Their number and scope remain vague: "Opus . . . alteri vel pluribus commisisse." The nature of the sources in the third decision is not specified beyond "written documents or oral traditions," and matters such as the number, dates and redaction of sources are not mentioned. Moreover this particular decree is of limited applicability, for what sources available to Moses are in fact determinable within the Pentateuch? The vagueness of the terms used throughout the decisions is apparent for example in the reference to all the results of nineteenth century Pentateuchal criticism as "argumenta a criticis congesta," and in the description of changes subsequent to the death of Moses as "non nullas modificationes."

Although the Commission left open the possibility of additional evidence it must be admitted that the decrees, for all practical purposes, reject any form of Wellhausenism. In its effort to check the indiscreet zeal of those who would rush headlong into the paths of rationalistic biblical scholarship, the Commission at the same time repressed Catholic attempts to meet Wellhausenism in its own bailiwick. Nonetheless, if the decrees slowed Catholic Pentateuchal criticism to a snail's pace and deprived the Church of fruitful works from her biblical scholars, they at the same time saved Catholic scriptural criticism from many embarrassments and perhaps from errors. Likewise the cautious directives kept Catholic scholars from contributing to the spate of irresponsible and bootless critical speculations current at the time.

## J. Touzard

The 1906 decrees, *Lamentabili* and *Pascendi* effected a rapid evacuation of the critical positions which Catholics, following Lagrange, had begun to maintain. Many exegetes of course did not always agree with Lagrange. In official echelons however Lagrange's early work was never disapproved. Later the threat of modernism caused a reversal of opinion, and a 1912 decree of the Biblical Commission cautioned against his writings. And although the statements of the Biblical Commission did allow a certain freedom to critics, it is nevertheless undeniable that they scarcely encouraged Catholic scholars to delve into the deep of

166

Pentateuchal problems. That fears were not ill founded is evident from the number of censures and condemnations issued by various Roman congregations in the next two decades. J. Touzard's *Moïse et Josué*,[11] the first comprehensive analysis of the documentary theory to appear after the 1906 decrees, received from the Congregation of the Holy Office the censure "not safe to be taught." In the light of this reproof it is interesting to examine Touzard's views in order to discover what they reveal about the attitude of Church authorities during these years.

Touzard's treatment of the documentary hypothesis is incidental to his principal query: what assurance is there that the Pentateuch and Jos give us a true history of Moses and Josue? Although he sees in Moses the point of departure for the religious, social, legislative, and national movements of the Israelites, as well as the font of literary activity recording them, Touzard nevertheless holds that it is useless to deny the merits of the documentary theory. He assigns J and E to the ninth and eighth centuries respectively, but recognizes that the strata contain many materials prior and subsequent to these dates. The chronology of P is more difficult; doubtless it received exilic and postexilic additions of midrashic intent. The renewal of the covenant at Moab gives the core of Dt; yet here again many later accretions are entailed, even down to the time of Josia.

In his presentation of the source theory Touzard appeals for a distinction between the undeniable facts of literary criticism and the system of historical criticism in favor of which the literary data are employed. His appeal went for the most part unheeded however since the impact of modernism was still being felt. But rapid advances in archeology and oriental linguistics soon amplified knowledge of the biblical milieu and necessitated a reassessment of both Catholic and non-Catholic critical positions. The easy presuppositions of Wellhausenism—skepticism regarding history, the principle of cultural and religious evolution, the isolation of Israel—gave way before the inelucta-

167

ble evidence supplied by archeology and the literatures of the Near East.

## Recent papal documents

### Divino afflante Spiritu

Recognizing the import of these advances for biblical studies, Pius XII issued in 1943 the encyclical *Divino afflante Spiritu*,[12] not only a permission but also an urgent invitation for exegetes to address themselves to the challenging problems of both testaments. The pontiff singled out for particular mention the study of "the peculiar character and circumstances of the sacred writer, the age in which he lived, the sources written and oral to which he had recourse and the forms of expression which he employed."[13] Among the interpreter's tasks the investigation of the literary forms is of prime significance, the more so since biblical genres are usually very different from our own by reason of time and culture. The encyclical also emphasized the importance of textual criticism in the light of progress made in the last half century.

### The reply to Cardinal Suhard

Despite the encouragement proffered by *Divino afflante Spiritu* critics felt hampered by the still operative decrees of 1906. In 1948 Cardinal Emmanuel Suhard of Paris presented two questions for examination by the Biblical Commission, both related to the earlier Pentateuchal pronouncements. The changed nuances in the atmosphere of scriptural research are discernible even in the form of the cardinal's queries. Whereas the 1906 decisions had treated Mosaic authenticity directly, the cardinal in 1948 inquired obliquely about the time of the documents in the Pentateuch. A 1909 decree of the Biblical Commission had dealt with the historicity of Gn 1–3; forty years later the needs of scholarship proposed the question in terms of the historicity of the entire prehistory—Gn 1–11—and its literary forms. Concerning these difficulties the Commission declined to add to its earlier pronouncements, recommending that the interpretation of the former decrees in the light of *Divino afflante Spiritu* would suffice to express the mind of the Church and grant proper freedom to the exegete.[14] The reply also cited a particular paragraph of the encyclical as a guideline for the scholar in his interpretation of the sacred writings:

The Catholic commentator . . . should in no way be deterred from grappling again and again with these difficult problems, hitherto unsolved, not only that he may refute the objections of adversaries, but also may attempt to find a satisfactory solution, which will be in full accord with the doctrine of the Church, . . . and which will at the same time satisfy the indubitable conclusions of profane sciences. Let all the other sons of the Church bear in mind that the efforts of these resolute laborers in the vineyard of the Lord should be judged not only with equity and justice, but also with the greatest charity; all, moreover, should abhor that intemperate zeal which imagines that whatever is new should for that reason be opposed or suspected.[15]

Although the Commission issued no new directives its comments tellingly disclose the new atmosphere of Catholic biblical research. For example the second of the 1906 decrees circumspectly grants that in the production of the Pentateuch Moses may have employed written documents or oral traditions; the time of these sources is not even touched on. Far different is the 1948 reply, which asserts: "There is no one today who doubts the existence of these sources or refuses to admit a progressive development of the Mosaic laws, . . . a development which is also manifest in the historical narratives."[17] The reply to Cardinal Suhard warns however that the nature and number of the documents, their denomination and dates, offer problems whose solution lies not so much in the diversity of the documents themselves as in the special psychology and thought processes of early oriental peoples and in the literary forms they used to express themselves. The question of the genres in the first eleven chapters of Gn, the reply continues, is obscure and complex; their analysis is rendered more difficult because they cannot be judged according to classical or modern styles. To interpret them aright the critic must follow an arduous path:

> The first duty here incumbent upon scientific exegesis consists before all in the attentive study of all the literary, scientific, historical, cultural and religious problems connected with these chapters; one should then examine closely the literary processes of the early Oriental peoples, their psychology, their way of expressing themselves and their very notion of historical truth; in a word, one should collate without prejudice all the subject matter of the paleontological and historical, epigraphic and literary sciences. Only thus can we hope to look more clearly into the true nature of certain narratives in the first Chapters of Genesis.[17]

Yet with all this labor many of the thornier problems cannot be given a positive solution. The Commission is nevertheless confident that if the exegete employs the methods of sound criticism, his study will doubtless establish the role of Moses both as author and lawgiver.

## Recent Catholic Pentateuchal studies

### Augustin Bea

The phenomenal strides made in archeology and oriental linguistics, which the Church acknowledged in *Divino afflante Spiritu* and in the reply to Cardinal Suhard, began to exert an ever increasing influence on Catholic criticism toward the end of the 1940s. Even before Pius XII's encyclical exegetes had begun to address themselves with new confidence to Pentateuchal studies, reshaping the traditional arguments and advancing hypotheses of their own. One of the first of these new treatments was Augustin (now Cardinal) Bea's *De Pentateucho*,[18] which has two concerns: the establishment of Mosaic authorship and the refutation of the documentary theory which denies this authorship. The substantial authenticity Bea seeks to confirm is not in the most rigorous sense, but in the sense proposed by theological sources of Scripture and tradition which, says Bea, affirm that Moses is the author of the Pentateuch.

Bea develops his refutation of the documentary hypothesis under three headings: philosophical, critico-literary and historico-archeological. The concept of religious and cultural evolution forming the philosophical basis of Wellhausenism Bea disposes of briefly: no Catholic can subscribe to this theory since it openly contradicts Catholic faith. Moreover evolutionism has been refuted by fact; monotheism for example does not necessarily develop from lower forms of animism and fetishism.

Wellhausenism rests its critico-literary arguments chiefly on the diversity in the divine names and on doublets; but neither of these phenomena, Bea claims, can establish the presence of various documents. From his study of the use of the divine names in the LXX and in the MT he concludes that the Greek does not always render the primitive text faithfully, and that the fidelity of the MT, although greater than that of the LXX, is not certain in every case. The examination of separate instances will reveal that psychological, linguistic, religious and literary considerations account for the use now of Yahweh, now of Elohim. As for doublets, positing documents to explain them transfers the difficulty from the author to the redactor. More probably the duplications stem from the nature of Semitic language and style, which evince a certain fondness for such a manner of speaking, and from the repetition natural to oral

171

transmission. Some duplicate passages give evidence of two distinct purposes on the part of the sacred writer. And it is possible that there is only the appearance of duplication when similar events occurring at different times are related in almost the same way.

Lastly Bea takes up the arguments directed against Pentateuchal historicity in general and against the historicity of Dt and the Priestly legislation in particular. Opposing the Wellhausen contention that geographic and chronological considerations preclude Moses' authorship, Bea offers evidence of the fidelity with which the Pentateuchal narratives report the conditions of their own age. In details like the names of the patriarchs and in the delineation of Egyptian life the narratives are consonant with what we know from profane sources of the same time. Dt demands special attention however because the assertion of its post-Mosaic origin is of vital moment in the evolutionary theory. The crux of the matter is the nature of the lawbook found in the Temple. Bea contends that no one can prove that it was Dt alone, and not the entire Pentateuch, which was discovered in 621. And even if it could be established that the book was Dt, lateness of composition would not necessarily follow. Actually Dt shows internal signs of early composition, and the conditions it describes reflect the time of entry into Canaan. The Wellhausen case for postexilic origin of P will not hold up either, for the legislation of the Priestly writer (known to Ezechiel and the Deuteronomist) does not always correspond to postexilic usages.

After thus devoting the major portion of his treatment to countering the position of the Wellhausen school, Bea undertakes a positive exposition of Pentateuchal origins. Following the 1906 decrees he readily concedes the possibility of Moses' use of sources, but he denies that these can be so nicely determined—much less identified—as J, E, D and P. Doubtless

172

Moses' work was based chiefly on oral traditions, but written records were probably available for the legislative portions. Although they no doubt underwent the accidental mutations common to all manuscripts in the course of transmission, the books of Moses, Bea maintains, were preserved with substantial integrity. As for Moses' role in their composition, in some instances he used extant documents, in other cases he added new ones of his own.

Bea's publications since *De Pentateucho* display a continued opposition to the documentary theory. True, he affirms that the work of the Catholic exegete is to determine Pentateuchal sources and the additions affixed to them, but he limits these sources to ones used by Moses himself.[19] Hence his examination of the present status of Pentateuchal studies is not so much a presentation of the positive gains made by new trends in criticism, especially form criticism, as it is a recital of the philosophical, historical and linguistic deficiencies of the source theory against which the new methods are directed. Although Bea sees in form criticism an ally against Wellhausenism the welcome he accords it is not completely enthusiastic, for as yet it has been more effective in demolishing old tenets than in offering new solutions. Furthermore its excessive attention to individual blocks of tradition causes a neglect of the personality of the sacred writer. Bea's reserve toward both Wellhausenism and form criticism seems a consequence of his very strict concept of the meaning of Mosaic authorship, even when it is considered substantially. Continued biblical research will indicate, he hopes, that a return to Moses and the ancient ways of viewing his role are in order.

## Paul Heinisch

In the introduction written for his translation of Gn in 1930[20] Paul Heinisch treats the Pentateuch in much the same manner as Bea does. After summarizing the evidence regarding Moses

173

as author he marshals the principal arguments for the postulation of documents in the Pentateuch and essays a brief refutation of each. Heinisch thinks it very probable that Moses, with the help of secretaries, composed both the primitive and patriarchal accounts from oral traditions. The laws first given by Moses were developed according to the changed circumstances of later days; but since they retained their original character and spirit they can truly be called a projection of Mosaic thought. In this regard Heinisch is more liberal than Bea, who would limit modifications in the legislative sections to the period between the promulgation of the law and the death of Moses.

## Alberto Vaccari

In the same decade, during the observance of Biblical Week in 1937, Alberto Vaccari proposed in an address before Pope Pius XI two recensions of the Pentateuch as a counterattack upon the documentary hypothesis and as a solution to the puzzle of the doublets.[21] Like Heinisch and Bea, Vaccari sees in the duplicates and the alternation in the use of the divine names the strongest evidence that several authors have been at work, and he wishes to give these factors due weight without at the same time prejudicing Mosaic authenticity. He points out that alternations and duplications are found elsewhere, e.g. in Pss, without the postulation of two or more authors. Consequently he feels that the entire Hebrew Bible manifests a kind of literary dualism (parallel to the political dualism of Jewish history and even closely akin to it) accompanied by alternation in the use of the divine names. Thus there are two collections in the psalter, two sets of proverbs of Solomon and two redactions of Jer.

If the same effects are products of the same causes, argues Vaccari, this similarity can be applied advantageously to Pentateuchal criticism. The Pentateuch, exclusively the work of

174

Moses, circulated in both Juda and Ephraim, absorbing in different milieux the variants which long ages of transmission, oral or written, customarily produce. Eventually the two currents diverging from a single source were united, though retaining the variations in language and style which had accrued. At times the two accounts were preserved side by side, as is the case with the story of creation. Less frequently the strands were interwoven, as in the account of the Flood. A parallel fusion is found in Tatian's *Diatessaron,* a blend of the four gospels. Combining the strands in the Pentateuch was a much simpler matter, thinks Vaccari, for a single original author and only two redactions are involved.

Vaccari's proposal has the advantage of being based on phenomena found in the rest of the Bible and thus can help solve difficult questions outside the Pentateuch. More importantly it maintains Mosaic authenticity and still allows for modifications which actually have occurred. Unfortunately however his theory is based largely on assumption and is of no value to the critic in determining Pentateuchal origins. For example the parallel which Vaccari draws between the J and E redactions and the two collections of psalms is not the slightest help in the documentary question, since no one would think of attributing one of the psalm redactions to errors in transmission. Vaccari tells us that these errors occurred in both oral and written transmission. But if the Pentateuch is, as he believes, completely the work of Moses, then his references to oral transmission can hardly be taken seriously. Finally one may ask: why only two redactions? Is this perhaps some law of textual criticism?

## Lagrange's last work

While the above-named works were being published, Lagrange maintained the silence into which he had lapsed at the time of the modernist crisis. He had however at no time retracted the views on the Pentateuch announced at Fribourg and Toulouse. In the last year of his life he again stated his opinion and enlisted a modified documentary theory in the service of Catholic exegesis.[22] He reasoned that since the Biblical Commission allowed sources and modifications in the Pentateuch the work of the Catholic exegete must be to discover their nature and extent, a task which the denial of the documentary theory cannot accomplish. Lagrange's interest was not in demonstrating the existence of sources but in suggesting the order and date of the strata J, E and P found in Gn.

Lagrange's proposed solution starts with Ex 3:13–15 (E), where God reveals his name, Yahweh, hitherto apparently unknown. At the same time he identifies himself with "the God of your fathers," Abraham, Isaac and Jacob. The later P text (Ex 6:2–4) attempts to harmonize the possible discrepancy by affirming: "I appeared to Abraham, Isaac, and Jacob as El Shadday, but under my name of Yahweh I did not reveal myself." The two texts show that for Abraham and his descendants El was a supreme, personal God who eventually revealed his true name: Yahweh. All critics agree, says Lagrange, that this name of God does not appear prior to the Sinai revelation. It seems logical that after its disclosure the sacred writers stopped using the name "El," except for special effect, as in certain psalms or in the Priestly writing; hence it is probable that accounts in which "El" figures are previous, at least in their sources, to Sinai. This fact, Lagrange believes, establishes not only the priority of the E document over J but also supplies E's latest possible date, the events of Sinai.

Traditions about the patriarchs in Canaan were doubtless preserved by Israel in Egypt and perhaps even written there as the E document. This source could have been one of those available to Moses, if he is not its author. Likewise he could have inspired

176

or written the post-Sinaitic document J. It is clear that Lagrange regards E as anterior to Sinai and J as posterior, but it is difficult to determine exactly how he relates Moses to the documents and to their redaction. The undeniable unity of Gn requires a single redactor, affirms Lagrange, and this redactor merits the name of author. The pre-existent elements the redactor used were parallel histories of a general nature, with differences stemming from their primitive oral character. These the redactor combined to achieve best his purpose: the portrayal of Yahweh's past intervention as an earnest of his future presence in favor of a people unified by their religious calling.

Lagrange does not assign a precise date to P, but notes that critical studies have established its Mosaic authenticity. And he is confident that the methods he utilizes in determining the date and order of E and J can be applied with the same results to the rest of the Pentateuch.

## Joseph Chaine

Lagrange's opinions about the documents in Gn were largely adopted by Joseph Chaine in his translation and commentary, *Le livre de la Genèse.*[23] This work reveals the new freedom experienced by biblical scholars after *Divino afflante Spiritu,* for, dispensing with a lengthy and cautious investigation of proofs supporting a documentary theory, Chaine announces simply that he recognizes three documents in Gn: J, E and P. Throughout the text he uses the sigla J, E and P as marginal indications of the origin of passages, and he appends to his commentary a description of the characteristics of each stratum. Chaine's concept of the documents is somewhat rigid and mechanical however and shows little concern for the oral traditions which had become a preoccupation of biblical criticism.

The dating of the sources and the determination of their place

177

of origin offer him a thornier problem. After reviewing the conclusions regnant in Wellhausen circles Chaine repeats Lagrange's arguments for the priority of E. P's redaction as we know it is later than Dt and represents the last stage of a developed legislation, many provisions of which—e.g. the distinction between clean and unclean animals—are very ancient. Progressive legislation, particularly that which applies to priestly duties, Chaine regards as an adaptation to a new era.

Besides subscribing to Lagrange's view of the documents in Gn, Chaine develops the Dominican's teaching on the divergence between the Semitic concept of history and that of the western world. An appreciation of this difference is essential if one is to understand the sacred writer. Again and again Chaine insists that certain pericopes are literary genres alien to history in the modern sense; one cannot demand of the author scientific historicity of detail, either in words or in deeds.

## Roland de Vaux

The role of tradition in the formation of the sacred writings has received due recognition in the Pentateuchal criticism found in the biblical translations and commentaries sponsored by L'École Biblique of Jerusalem. Roland de Vaux in his general introduction to the Pentateuch acknowledges the activity of several writers—betrayed by marked contrasts in language, style and viewpoint.[24] Yet the Pentateuch cannot be regarded as a mechanical compilation of written sources; rather the facts require recognition that traditions or cycles of tradition have been united in the final redaction. Thus the word "tradition" becomes the hallmark of Pentateuchal criticism in the Jerusalem Bible: one does not speak of documents but of traditions. De Vaux does not define the term but his meaning can be inferred and his view substantiated from his other writings.

178

De Vaux groups the traditions according to affinities of language, concepts and constants, such as that of the usage of the divine names, which determine the parallel lines found throughout the Pentateuch. The same criteria employed in literary criticism determine the cycles of tradition, but they are applied more flexibly and without the literary critic's concern for chronology. After all, if the components of the Pentateuch are traditions showing parallel development then the date of their definitive constitution, perhaps achieved only after long years of oral and written evolution, can be stated only approximately. De Vaux assigns J to the reign of Solomon; E, slightly later. The date of Dt can be determined by its relation to the reforms of Josia, though it gives evidence of material prior and subsequent to that time. The Priestly tradition was constituted as such during the Exile, and its laws were not imposed until after the return.

For the milieu of each tradition de Vaux looks to the sanctuaries where Yahweh's mighty deeds were recalled and extolled on festal occasions. Connection with a sanctuary is more readily established, he believes, for the legal sections than for the narrative. The Judean origin of J can be inferred from the prominence it gives to Hebron and from the leading role it accords Juda in the Joseph story. De Vaux assigns a northern provenance to E but in its case the evidence is not so compelling. D appears to represent, at least in its basic elements, the northern customs brought to Jerusalem by the Levites after the fall of Samaria in 722. The Priestly tradition on the other hand derives from the Temple priests at Jerusalem. De Vaux concludes that ascertaining the approximate date and provenance of the traditions still tells relatively little about their primitive origins and forms.

Despite the characteristics distinguishing the traditions de Vaux avers that they are not independent but have a common origin. Their political and social conditions, their geographic

179

and historical forms do not correspond to those of the era in which the traditions supposedly were constituted. The findings of archeology and oriental texts indicate that the events described actually occurred in a much earlier age, at the time when Israel was formed as a people. The same can be said, with certain reservations, for the legislative sections. Without doubt the various codes show a difference in spirit—the result of milieu or change in circumstances or ideas—but basic to each code are the same juridic principles, the same religion, the same cult. While developing in accord with the needs of the people governed, the laws always retained their ancient provisions. The common origin of the traditions and the unity of the books into which they were incorporated, de Vaux insists, demand recognition of the singular role of Moses in the formation of the Pentateuch. Certain narratives and legislative portions date to the time when Israel was constituted as a people, and this epoch was dominated by the figure of Moses as organizer, religious leader and legislator. It is Moses' historic role which tradition primarily expresses in attributing to him the Pentateuch; less firm however is the tradition which assigns to Moses the actual redaction of the books.

## Henri Cazelles

The separate volumes of the Jerusalem Bible unfold additional views on the nature and beginnings of the Pentateuch. Doubtless his studies of Israelite law have shaped the ideas Henri Cazelles, one of the collaborators, presents in the introductions to his translations of Lv, Nm and Dt.[25] Although Cazelles disclaims that he is propounding a specific system his remarks can be synthesized into a coherent theory of Pentateuchal origins. He posits the documents, J, E, P and D in that order of time but warns, as does de

Vaux, against a purely mechanical concept of the writings. A document is after all a synthesis, a collection, not a creation. Yet these documents (whose true nature is more precisely indicated by the words "traditions" or "currents" are not sufficient to explain the Pentateuch. Cazelles finds the final conflation of all the traditions stamped with the seal of Moses not only in form but in basic content as well.

Most critics who thus testify to Mosaic authenticity tread lightly when there is question of assigning passages to Moses or even to his era. Cazelles shows similar prudence, yet he does not hesitate to attribute the Decalogue and the statutes in Ex 21:1ff to Moses. The chronology of these individual passages however is not so delicate a matter as dating the strata P and D, whose final redaction can be determined with only relative certainty. Yet Cazelles does discover some helpful indications: the Levitical synthesis of law supposes an agricultural life and long contact with Canaan—in fine, a culture hardly expected of a people that lives in the desert. The laws of the Priestly code then must have been formulated only after the settlement in Canaan. Can the date be focused more clearly? Cazelles' attempt to relate much of P to the time and influence of Ezechiel leads to three conclusions. First, many elements in Lv are anterior to Ezechiel (the scroll of Ez 2:9 was doubtless the Law of Holiness [Lv 17–26]). Second, the provisions of the sacrificial laws, found in Ez but not in any prior historical or prophetical books, argue for the direct influence of Ezechiel in the formation of Lv. Similarities in style, vocabulary and theological concerns also point to this influence. Third, some laws are posterior to Ezechiel: the stipulations of Lv 1–8, used even in the first century after Christ, represent an advance upon the Torah of Ezechiel (Ez 40–48).

Almost all scholars agree that the D document was not written at one sitting, but the exact time and place of its composition are causes for disagreement. Cazelles holds that parts of Dt arose in northern circles among the Levites since the ministers of the north would be interested in securing equal rights for all priests. The time of their coming to Jerusalem, around 700, would also correspond to the establishment of a central cult. Cazelles thinks that after the Exile a second redaction of Dt occurred and additional chapters were inserted with a more precise view of exile as a punishment for infidelity (see for example Dt 4:25–31).

## Albert Clamer

The lengthy general introduction to the Pentateuch which Albert Clamer gives to his translation of Gn[26] summarizes the traditions about Mosaic authorship, the origins and bases of the documentary theory, new developments in Catholic and non-Catholic criticism and pertinent directives of the magisterium. Clamer seems content however with setting forth the views of others (especially those contained in *La Sainte Bible de Jérusalem*) and then indicating, in a very general way, the lines Catholic Pentateuchal criticism should follow. Literary analysis has confirmed a number of facts whose most reasonable explanation is supplied by a theory of documents, sources or traditions. From the conflation of these latter the Pentateuch resulted. If the admission of documents leads to the assertion that the books as we know them are not the work of Moses, it must yet be admitted that the composition of the documents is not so late as many critics aver and that many of the historical traditions and laws incorporated in them are Mosaic or even pre-Mosaic. Dating back to the very origins of Israel, they cannot be separated from the person of Moses, the organizer of Israel's national and religious life.

182

## Albin van Hoonacker

It is noteworthy that whereas German scholarship has made the most important contributions to biblical studies in non-Catholic circles, it is the French who have made the chief advances among Catholics. But the name of a Belgian, Albin van Hoonacker, professor at Louvain, is not to be omitted. Among the scriptural studies he published in his lifetime Pentateuchal criticism as such does not figure, but almost twenty years after his death there appeared his treatise *De compositione et de origine Mosaica Hexateuchi disquisitio historico-critica,* an analysis of the Hexateuch with a view to determining its literary composition and origin.[27] The writing of the undated manuscript can with probability be assigned to the years between 1896 and 1908. Considering the progress of biblical studies in the forty years between the composition and publication of this work, it is no surprise that *De compositione* leaves untouched questions and methods which have become vital to scriptural research. Especially conspicuous is the total neglect of form criticism. It is nevertheless surprising that so early a study anticipates the analyses and conclusions of later scholars. A reason for van Hoonacker's failure to publish the disquisition is readily found: modernism was in the air and official pronouncements made the time unpropitious for issuing one's critical findings. That van Hoonacker was in advance of his age can be seen from the freshness and cogency which his criticism, within limits, still has.

Van Hoonacker concludes that Scripture and tradition do not proffer compelling testimony of Mosaic authorship, but they do testify unanimously to Moses' role in the promulgation of the law. The *pièce de resistance* of van Hoonacker's work is an investigation of the sacred writings to determine what independent documents were used in their composition. Here and in later fields of investigation his method is to look first at the legislative

183

sections and then at the narrative. In the law codes he finds variations even in legislation dealing with the same general subject matter. Some provisions suppose groups dwelling in the desert; others, a people settled in Canaan. These anomalies suggest that the present codes involved more than one author. By a painstaking collation and analysis of laws touching altar, feasts and priestly affairs van Hoonacker confirms this thesis.

Van Hoonacker makes a similar examination of the narrative sections for traces of their basic documents. From the amassed evidence he draws the critical conclusion that four documents exist in the Hexateuch. Yet even when these are admitted the lack of homogeneity within a given document raises further difficulties. Heterogeneity is of two kinds: that which stems from the presence of subdocuments or of erratic blocks and that which results from redactional mutations.

The Belgian's careful analysis of the legislative and narrative sections also enables him to draw some conclusions about the age of the documents. Certain subdocuments, such as Gn 14 and 49, are obviously pre-Mosaic. The antiquity of much of the other material is attested indirectly through parallels furnished by institutions and literary traditions of the Near East. Countering objections brought against the pre-exilic formation of P and D, van Hoonacker holds that the legislation of both P and D existed independently before being conflated in the Pentateuch. Moreover Dt shows great affinities to the Code of the Covenant (Ex 20–23) and to the Law of Holiness (Lv 17–26), both of which are acknowledged to be of great age; hence Dt may be regarded as a fresh promulgation of ancient Mosaic law.

Van Hoonacker finds the question of Moses' role in the composition of the documents more difficult than any of the preceding problems. The difficulty can be solved only indirectly. The definite attribution of a passage to Moses, e. g. the Canticle of Moses (Dt 33), is not sufficient to guarantee authenticity.

What we know of the Hebrew practice of assigning great men as authors of new pieces forbids us to settle the matter so simply. Yet the most ancient traditions all affirm that the covenant was negotiated by Moses and that it was in his time that the fundamental religious and cultural institutions of Israel were founded. Tradition assigns all laws, even new ones, to Moses as their promulgator. This attitude views him as the writer of the law and presupposes the common tradition that he was not only an oral legislator but an author as well.

As for Moses' activity in writing the Pentateuch, van Hoonacker continues, it can only be said that his was not the final redaction, nor yet the first one, for this revision was made in Canaan, not in the desert. Not even the individual documents are properly called Mosaic; the presence of many post-Mosaic elements prevents this claim. What solution then does van Hoonacker propose? Only that the Pentateuch displays certain Mosaic elements combined with many other materials anterior and posterior to Moses' time. He sums up the conclusions of his analysis under two headings: first, the presence of documents and subdocuments in the Hexateuch cannot be doubted; second, the role of Moses in the composition of the primary sources of the legislation and narratives demands that he be recognized as the substantial author of the Hexateuch.

## Joseph Coppens

Van Hoonacker's student and successor at Louvain, Joseph Coppens, has not published a complete statement of his own ideas about the origins of the Books of Moses, but no summary of Catholic Pentateuchal criticism can omit his name. One of his most outstanding works is a comprehensive study of Old Testament criticism, a work which is primarily concerned with the Pentateuch.[28] His position for many years as editor of the section "Chronique de l'Ancien Testament" in ETL has given

185

Coppens frequent opportunities to express his views about the Pentateuch; many of his most trenchant observations have been made as *obiter dicta* in his critiques of Pentateuchal research. However Coppens' theory of the Pentateuch is somewhat in flux; his opinion of yesterday is not necessarily what he holds today. Nevertheless he has consistently followed the paths traced by "notre chèr maître," Albin van Hoonacker, and he frequently reminds the subjects of his criticisms that they would do well to walk in like manner.

From this survey of the biblical research of Catholic scholars can be seen the happy results of *Divino afflante Spiritu* and the reply to Cardinal Suhard. Some scholars unfortunately are unaware of the new dimension in biblical criticism; certain of them have ignored the recommendations of Pius XII to utilize the findings of archeology, literature and linguistics in exegesis. Others show themselves conversant with the latest research; they apply its results not scientifically but according to their own presuppositions. A case in point is Bonaventura Mariani in his *Introductio in Libros Sacros Veteris Testamenti.*[29] His lengthy bibliographies and abundant notes witness the greatest familiarity with contemporary archeology, linguistics and literary criticism; yet his presentation of this wealth of material ultimately fails to advance our understanding of the Bible. Rather it provides him with targets (as regards the Pentateuch) in his refutation of the documentary theory. He sees in almost every non-Catholic critic an adversary to be refuted, not a coworker from whom to learn.

## Summary and conclusions

The above survey indicates that an understanding of the Pentateuch and its place in salvation history is impossible without consideration of the manifold sources from which it has been composed. The concept of these strata has altered radically since they were first accepted in the nineteenth century. Originally determined exclusively by literary criticism, the sources were judged creations of individual authors and, despite the presence of admittedly ancient materials, were generally assigned to the age when they were first committed to writing. Subsequently an appreciation of oral tradition among the Semites and a keener understanding of the biblical milieu (the result chiefly of archeological research and progress in oriental studies) enabled form criticism to go beyond literary analysis, to penetrate the sources and to establish individual components of the strands J, E, D and P. Modern criticism has thus afforded a freer, more pliant concept of the sources as independent oral and written traditions long current among the Hebrews, traditions constantly absorbing new elements before their definitive constitution. The documents, insofar as they can be determined, are collections, not creations, syntheses of traditions arising at various times and in different milieux. As to the further nature of the sources—their origin, date and process of growth—critics hold widely divergent opinions.

Although as early as 1906 the Biblical Commission had conceded that Moses may have selectively employed written documents or oral traditions in the production of his work, the Commission was less willing to admit sources later than Moses, contending that critical arguments are not sufficiently cogent to justify the assertion that the Pentateuch was compiled from sources for the most part posterior to Moses. Gradually however Catholic critics have come to accept the source theory as a reasonable working hypothesis for understanding the Pentateuch, so that at the present time almost all admit both the sources and the progressive development of the legislation and narratives they contain. With the decline of nineteenth century concomitants of the documentary theory—rationalism, Hegelianism, evolutionism, historicism—Catholic scholars have evinced a greater readiness to apply the methods and to accept some of the conclusions of non-Catholic biblical scholarship. Consequently one cannot speak of a specifically Catholic theory of the Pentateuch.

Now that the respective realms of literary and form criticism have been clarified, their merits and deficiencies recognized, it would seem that a judicious use of critical methods will finally lead to a satisfactory solution of the problem concerning Pentateuchal origins and development. Yet despite genuine progress, the cumulative result of many painstaking studies, there is no consensus among scholars. It can even be said that Pentateuchal research, rather than being united in its common pursuit, is in a state of flux. Literary criticism has been pushed to its limits; form criticism still has a long way to go before its analysis of individual pericopes is complete, but even this feat will not be the final word of wisdom. Both critical methods have concentrated on isolated, partial elements to such an extent that the context—the definitive form of the Pentateuch—has been lost to view. The minute examination of a literary form has little to tell us about the Books of Moses in their present state, and labeling some of its narratives "etiological legends" makes the structure of Gn no clearer.

Analysis, both literary and form, is essential. But analysis must be followed by synthesis, and here lies the difficulty: how is the coalescence of so many divergent elements in the Pentateuch to be explained? Extensive complexes of legends permeate the Mosaic writings, and point to collectors of narratives and perhaps to localizations of stories in cultic sanctuaries. The traditional material so preserved formed the foundation of larger collections. The agreement between biblical accounts and extrabiblical sources of known date permits the judgment that the early traditions were passed along substantially intact. This continuity of tradition throughout the centuries requires explanation. What dictated the preservation of a tradition in the first place? What theological program imposed the laws of its development? On these points critics of the Pentateuch are often unaccountably silent.

Unlike twentieth century scholars the exegetes of the last century were unembarrassed by committing themselves to a definite theory on the nature of the Hebrew religion, since Wellhausenism provided them with a ready-made explanation of Yahwism. Their critical orthodoxy rested on a twofold basis: analysis of the documents and an evolutionary theory about the development of Hebrew religion. Both of these pillars have now been shaken. The inadequacies of the documentary hypothesis have been partially supplied for by form criticism. But what has replaced the evolutionist concept of Yahwism?

So long as religion was interpreted according to Hegelian immanentism the task of the Old Testament theologian differed little from that of the historian; he had only to record phenomenological data, assuming that the reality to which the Old Testament bears witness can be grasped and comprehended by historical means. As a result of the evolutionist explication of Israel's gradual realization of Yahweh, theology became subservient to history; or rather theology and the history of Israelite religion were identified. Evolutionism, the philosophic rationale of critical orthodoxy, has now been laid to rest and as yet biblicists have proposed no generally accepted theory to take its place. Because of an exaggerated concern for scientific objectivity in biblical studies critics often ignore the elements of inexplicability in the religion of the Hebrews, even though they may be uneasily aware that scientific research alone cannot account for the religious experience recorded in Scripture. The interpreter of the sacred writings cannot manage without a view of Hebrew religion which will elucidate those factors beyond the reach of scientific analysis.

Efforts to construct such a view are not lacking. E. A. Speiser for example argues that Israel's unique treatment of history is fully explicable only in terms of her religion, because the living torah of the historical materials contains a design for a divinely appointed way of life.[30] The perseverance of tradition among the Hebrews can be accounted for by positing a canon composed of traditions illustrating the theme of Israel's special relation to Yahweh. More than a chronicle, Hebrew history transcends and transfigures the facts it relates by showing the hand of Yahweh directing Israel to her destiny. While the narratives were being successively implemented the compilers never lost sight of the true nature of their work—the recording of Israel's meeting with Yahweh and life in his presence. The actions dealt with were circumscribed in time and place but their ultimate significance was timeless and universal.

The final canon shows that interpretative history was a subject of supreme importance. Can it be determined when such a persuasion took hold? Speiser believes that the conviction arose when the traditions were still in oral form, perhaps at the time of the patriarchs themselves; the conviction effected a canon of traditions calculated to serve the over-all concept of Yahweh working in history. Canonicity implies sanctity, and sanctity in turn supposes that some vital importance is attached to the traditions precisely because they clarify the relations between Yahweh and his people. Since he was dealing with a canon of tradition the compiler was not free to manipulate or recast his materials, even when their significance was no longer clear to him. Setting down incomprehensible details can only mean that the narrator's duty was to record and pass on what tradition had handed down to him; to retell, not to originate. The sacred writers viewed the traditions with awe and passed them along in a continuous line as embodiments of the divine plan for Israel's way of life, an ideal not granted to the other nations.

Speiser's work is primarily an explanation of the biblical concept of history; it is also relevant to the problem of Hebrew religion in general, since in Yahweh's saving plan revelation and history are intimately related. That modern critics sense the need for implementation of literary and historical studies is apparent in the resurgence of biblical theology in non-Catholic circles. Scholars are coming to realize that the key question in Old Testament research is: does it suffice for the biblical critic to be a literary and historical expert, or must he also be a theologian in order to interpret the Scriptures fully?

Catholics have long known what non-Catholics are gradually realizing: theological commitment need not disqualify a man as an objective, scientific critic of Scripture. No complete synthesis of the Pentateuch seems possible at this time; but with the commitment of faith aided by modern techniques of research the Catholic critic can make ever greater advances in elucidating the Bible, for "this true liberty of the children of God, which adheres faithfully to the teaching of the Church and accepts and uses gratefully the contributions of profane sciences, this liberty, upheld and sustained by the confidence of all, is the condition and source of all solid progress in Catholic doctrine."[31]

191

# Footnotes to Chapter 3

[1] See Joseph Coppens, *The Old Testament and the Critics*, tr by E. A. Ryan and E. W. Tribbe (Paterson, N.J. 1942); C. R. North, "Pentateuchal Criticism," *The Old Testament and Modern Study*, ed H. H. Rowley (Oxford 1951) 48–83; or any recent Old Testament introduction, such as Aage Bentzen, *Introduction to the Old Testament*, 2 vol, 2d ed (Copenhagen 1952).

[2] For the key points of Wellhausen's theory see *Prolegomena to the History of Ancient Israel*, tr Menzies and Black (New York 1957) 1–13; for an analysis of the Hexateuchal narratives, 297–362.

Hegel's philosophy is based on the realization of the Absolute which is Spirit. The full realization of Spirit is Spirit's knowledge of itself. This self-knowledge occurs through a dialectical development, beginning with a thesis (a primitive state of reality of Idea), countered by antithesis (a more developed state of reality or Nature), from which evolves a synthesis (a higher state of reality or finite spirits).

History, according to Hegel, is whatever happens. As such it is the unfolding of the Absolute, the Divine Idea realizing itself. The first stage is the advent of Nature, culminating in the production of man or finite spirit. In the second state of development man comes to know himself and Nature, and to know that these are different from each other. Finally man in knowing Nature comes to know the Absolute as realized in both Nature and himself. This is the full realization of the Absolute: Infinite Spirit realized through finite spirits knowing themselves in Nature and finite spirits. Man's knowledge of the Absolute, or Spirit, Hegel calls the philosophy of history, which again develops dialectically until it reaches the synthesis of religious consciousness. Religion, as Hegel conceives it, is imagery or art enhanced with thought.

Hegel's philosophy of religion consists of the development of man's knowledge of God. God's existence in himself is succeeded by man's knowledge of himself as finite and God as infinite; in the final stage man realizes himself as a finite being in God who is infinite. Hegel finds that the history of religion exemplifies his dialectic. In primitive religion God was conceived as immanent in Nature. In the antithetical phase of religion God was conceived as a transcendent Spirit and as individual person to whom man owes obedience and sacrifice—a fact exemplified in Jewish, Greek and Roman religion. In the third phase religion is absolute. This is Christianity, in which God is known as he actually is—Infinite Spirit, at once transcendent, as a

Trinity of Persons having infinite spiritual life, and immanent in Nature through Christ, who communicates divine life to men.

3 Few of the proposals concerning additional documents have met with favor. Among them are Otto Eissfeldt's *Laien* source (L), found in his *Hexateuch-Synopse* (Leipzig 1922); Julius Morgenstern's Kenite source (K), discussed in "The Oldest Document of the Hexateuch," HUCA 4 (1927) 1–138; and R. H. Pfeiffer's Seïr or Edomite source (S), in "A Non-Israelite Source of the Book of Genesis," ZAW 48 (1930) 66–73.

4 Gunkel expounded his theory of form criticism in *Reden und Aufsätze* (Göttingen 1913). See also *Schöpfung und Chaos* (Göttingen 1895); and *The Legends of Genesis,* tr W. H. Carruth (Chicago 1901).

5 See Henri Cazelles, "Mythe et l'Ancien Testament," VDBS 5 (1957) 240–52; or John L. McKenzie, "Myth and the Old Testament," CBQ 21 (1959) 265–82.

6 His talks were published as "Les sources de Pentateuque," RB 7 (1898) 10–32.

7 This book comprises lectures given at the Institut Catholique in Toulouse; a translation from the second edition appears as *Historical Criticism and the Old Testament,* tr Edward Meyers (London 1905).

8 The exegete's attempt to portray the process of dogmatic development frequently meets with objections from theologians. In a still pertinent passage Lagrange analyzes the tension:

"What disagreement there is comes from the different aims of the theologian and the historian. The theologian seeks light, full light; he is ever calling for more light. . . . He is the first to recognize the development of dogma, but what he fails to grasp is, why the knowledge of the fully-developed doctrine should not be made use of to the better understanding of the doctrine in its embryonic or primitive stage. Such a course, in his eyes, is little short of a sin against the light, for one cannot have too much light to see by.

On the other hand, the historian would reply that such was not his aim; that he wished to know, not all that dogma comprises at the present day, but what it included at a given epoch. As for himself, he would not refuse to use the light cast by the theologian, but that, as he was anxious to know what could be seen in that chamber a thousand years ago, he proposed to let down the blinds, as they were down then, and so to realize what could be made out. Present-day light will be of further use in showing clearly how that has sprung from this, and thus prove that this contained that; yet although we may realize the fact in the light of to-day, it does not follow that it could have been thought of in the past; and what we are really seeking is the amount of light shed by a particular opinion at a given period (ibid, 61–62).

9 *Pascendi,* ASS 40 (1907) 608. A summary of the encyclical can be found in Anne Freemantle (ed), *The Papal Encyclicals in Their Historical Context* (New York 1956) 197–201.

10 ASS 39 (1906) 377–78; and RSS, ed Conrad Louis, 118–19. Pius X stated the binding forces of these decrees in his motu proprio *Praestantia*

*Scripturae Sacrae,* ASS 40 (1907) 724. For more recent interpretation see Edward F. Siegman, "The Decrees of the Pontifical Biblical Commission: A Recent Clarification," CBQ 18 (1956) 23–29.

[11] DAFC 3 (1919) 695–755.

[12] AAS 35 (1943) 297–325; and RSS, 80–107, from which subsequent quotations are taken.

[13] ibid, 97.

[14] AAS 40 (1948) 45–48; and RSS, 150–53.

[15] ibid, 150–51.

[16] ibid, 151. The freedom which the reply concedes exegetes was sometimes abused. Pius XII protested a too literal interpretation of the directives in his *Humani generis* (AAS 42 [1950] (576–77). The letter to Cardinal Suhard does not lay down a program, but merely answers two particular questions.

[17] RSS, 152.

[18] (Rome 1933).

[19] See for example "Der heutige Stand der Pentateuchfrage," Bib 16 (1935) 175–200; and "Der heutige Stand der Bibelwissenschaft," SZ 153 (1953–54) 91–104.

[20] *Das Buch Genesis,* HSAT 1 (Bonn 1930).

[21] Vaccari's paper, "La questione mosaica e la filologia," was reported in *L'Osservatore Romano,* Sept. 24, 1937. It is partially printed in VD 17 (1937) 371–73. Vaccari prefaces his main subject with a demonstration of the inaccuracy of assigning a late date to the books of the Pentateuch. Philological analysis of the Masoretic text, the Septuagint and the Samaritan Pentateuch shows that the Pentateuch was transmitted by the Jews in the script used before the Exile, not in postexilic Aramaic. Since the Samaritans received the Pentateuch in the seventh century, there can be no question of exilic or postexilic composition of the Priestly writing. Dt is not late in origin either; all the forms in the Samaritan version manifest traces of long transmission.

[22] "L'authenticité mosaïque de la Genèse et la théorie des documents," RB 47 (1938) 163–83.

[23] (Paris 1951). This posthumous work was written before the reply to Cardinal Suhard in 1948.

[24] *La Genèse,* 2d ed, La sainte Bible de Jérusalem (Paris 1950).

[25] Cazelles' law studies include *Études sur la Code de l'Alliance* (Paris 1946) and "Loi israélite," VDBS 5 (1957) 497–530. His biblical translations are *Le Deutéronome, Le Lévitique* and *Les Nombres,* 2d ed, La Sainte Bible de Jérusalem (Paris 1958).

[26] *La Genèse* (Paris 1953) 9–76.

[27] Ed Joseph Coppens (Brussels 1949).

[28] *The Old Testament and the Critics.*

[29] (Rome 1958).

[30] "The Biblical Idea of History in Its Common Near Eastern Setting," IsrEJ 7 (1957) 201–16. See also George E. Mendenhall, "Biblical History in Transition," *The Bible and the Ancient Near East,* 39–40.

[31] Pius XII, *Divino afflante Spiritu,* RSS, 102.

# Bibliography

## Books

Alt, Albrecht. *Kleine Schriften zur Geschichte des Volkes Israel,* 3 vol, Munich, vols I and II, 1953, vol III, ed Martin Noth, 1959.

————. *Die Ursprünge des israelitischen Rechts* (Leipzig 1934). Printed also in *Kleine Schriften,* I, 278–332.

Albright, William F. *The Archaeology of Palestine,* rev ed (Baltimore 1960).

————. *From the Stone Age to Christianity: Monotheism and the Historical Process,* 2d ed (New York 1957).

————. *History, Archaeology and Christian Humanism* (New York 1963).

Baltzer, Klaus. *Das Bundesformular,* Wissenschaftliche Monographien zum Alten und Neuen Testament (Neukirchen Kreis Moers 1960).

Baron, Salo Wittmayer. *A Social and Religious History of the Jews,* 8 vol, 2d ed (Philadelphia 1952–58).

Bea, Augustin. *De Pentateucho* (Rome 1933).

Bentzen, Aage. *Introduction to the Old Testament,* 2 vol, 2d ed (Copenhagen 1952).

Briggs, Charles and von Hügel, Baron Friedrich. *The Papal Commission and the Pentateuch* (London 1906).

Beyerlin, W. *Herkunft und Geschichte der ältesten Sinaitradition* (Tübingen 1961).

Bright, John. *Early Israel in Recent History Writing,* Studies in Biblical Theology 19 (London 1956).

————. *A History of Israel* (Philadelphia 1959).

Buber, Martin. *Moses* (London 1946).

Cazelles, Henri. *Le Deutéronome,* La Sainte Bible de Jérusalem, 2d ed (Paris 1958).

————. *Études sur le Code de l'Alliance* (Paris 1946).

————. *Le Lévitique,* La Sainte Bible de Jérusalem, 2d ed (Paris 1958).

————. *Les Nombres,* La Sainte Bible de Jérusalem, 2d ed (Paris 1958).

———— *et al. Moïse, l'homme de l'Alliance* (Paris 1955).

Chaine, Joseph. *Le livre de la Genèse,* Lectio divina 3 (Paris 1951).

Clamer, Albert. *La Genèse* (Paris 1953).

Coppens, Joseph. *The Old Testament and the Critics,* tr E. A. Ryan and E. W. Tribbe (Paterson 1942).

Couroyer, B. *L'Exode,* La Sainte Bible de Jérusalem, 2d ed (Paris 1958).

Daniélou, Jean. *From Shadows to Reality: Studies in the Biblical Typology of the Fathers,* tr Wulfstan Hibberd (Westminster 1960).

Dentan, Robert, *et al. The Idea of History in the Ancient Near East,* American Oriental Series 38 (New Haven 1955).

Dubarle, A. M. *Le péché originel dans l'Écriture,* Lectio divina 20 (Paris 1958).

Eichrodt, Walther. *Theology of the Old Testament,* vol 1, tr from 6th German ed (1959) by John Baker (London 1961).

Eissfeldt, Otto. *Einleitung in das Alte Testament,* 2d ed (Tübingen 1956).

————. *Die Genesis der Genesis: Vom Werdegang des ersten Buches der Bibel* (Tübingen 1958).

————. *Hexateuch-Synopse: Die Erzählung der fünf Bücher Moses und des Buches Josua mit dem Anfange des Richtersbuches* (Leipzig 1922).

*Enchiridion biblicum,* 2d ed (Rome 1954).

Engnell, Ivan. *Studies in Divine Kingship in the Ancient Near East* (Uppsala 1943).

de Fraine, Jean. *The Bible and the Origin of Man,* tr from the Dutch (New York 1962).

Frankfort, H., and H. A. (eds) *The Intellectual Adventure of Ancient Man* (Chicago 1946).

Freemantle, Anne. (ed) *The Papal Encyclicals in Their Historical Context* (New York 1956).

Gressmann, Hugo. *Altorientalische Texte und Bilder zum Alten Testament,* 2 vol, 2d ed (Berlin 1927).

Grollenberg, L. H. *Atlas of the Bible,* tr and ed Joyce M. H. Reid and H. H. Rowley (Edinburgh 1956).

Guillet, Jacques. *Themes of the Bible,* tr Albert Mothe (Notre Dame 1960).

Gunkel, Hermann. *Genesis übersetzt und erklärt* (HAT. Göttingen 1902).

————. *The Legends of Genesis,* tr W. H. Carruth (Chicago 1901).

————. *Reden und Aufsätze* (Göttingen 1913).

————. *Schöpfung und Chaos in Urzeit und Endzeit* (Göttingen 1895).

Heidel, Alexander. *The Babylonian Genesis* (Chicago 1942).

————. *The Gilgamesh Epic and Old Testament Parallels* (Chicago 1946).

Heinisch, Paul. *Das Buch Genesis* (HSAT I. Bonn 1930).

Hempel, Johannes. *Die althebraische Literatur und ihr hellenistisch-judisches Nachleben* (Wildpark-Potsdam 1930).

Hooke, S. H. (ed) *Myth, Ritual, and Kingship: Essays on the Theory and Practice of Kingship in the Ancient Near East and in Israel* (Oxford 1958).

van Hoonacker, Albin. *De compositione litteraria et de origine mosaica Hexateuchi disquisitio historico-critica,* ed Joseph Coppens (Bruges 1949).

Kaufmann, Yehezkel. *The Religion of Israel: From Its Beginnings to the Babylonian Exile,* tr and ab Moshe Greenberg (Chicago 1960).

Kraus, Hans-Joachim. *Geschichte der historisch-kritischen Erforschung des Alten Testaments von der Reformation bis zur Gegenwart* (Neukirchen Kreis Moers 1956).

Lagrange, M. Joseph. *Historical Criticism and the Old Testament,* tr from 2d French ed by Edward Meyers (London 1905).

Lecuyer, J. (ed) *Abraham notre père* (Paris 1955).

Louis, Conrad. (ed) *Rome and the Study of Scripture,* 7th ed (St. Meinrad, Ind. 1962).

Mariani, Bonaventura. *Introductio in Libros Sacros Veteris Testamenti* (Rome 1958).

McKenzie, John L. (ed) *The Bible in Contemporary Catholic Thought* (New York 1962).

————. *Myths and Realities* (Milwaukee 1963).

————. *The Two-Edged Sword* (Milwaukee 1956).

Mendenhall, George E. *Law and Covenant in Israel and the Ancient*

197

*Near East* (Pittsburgh 1955). This was first published as "Ancient Oriental and Biblical Law," and "Covenant Forms in Israelite Tradition," BA 17 (1954) 22–46 and 49–76.

Mowinckel, Sigmund. *The Old Testament as the Word of God,* tr Reider B. Bjornard (Nashville 1959).

————. *Prophecy and Tradition: Prophetic Books in the Light of the Study and Growth of the History of Traditions* (Oslo 1946).

Muilenburg, James. *The Way of Israel: Biblical Faith and Ethics* (New York 1961).

Muñoz Iglesias, Salvador. (ed) *Doctrina pontificia, I: Documentos biblicos* (Madrid 1955).

North, Christopher R. *The Old Testament Interpretation of History* (London 1954).

Noth, Martin. *Exodus,* tr J. S. Bowden (London 1962).

————. *Die Gesetze im Pentateuch* (Halle 1940).

————. *The History of Israel,* rev ed, tr P. R. Ackroyd (New York 1960).

————. *Das System der zwölf Stämme Israels* (Stuttgart 1930).

————. *Überlieferungsgeschichte des Pentateuch* (Stuttgart 1948).

Oesterreicher, John M. (ed) *The Bridge, I: A Yearbook of Judaeo-Christian Studies* (New York 1955).

————. *The Bridge, III: A Yearbook of Judaeo-Christian Studies* (New York 1958).

Otto, Rudolf. *The Idea of the Holy: An Inquiry into the Non-Rational Factor in the Idea of the Divine and Its Relation to the Rational,* tr John W. Harvey (London 1923), 1936 printing.

Parrot, Andre. *The Tower of Babel,* Studies in Biblical Archaeology 2 (London 1955).

Pedersen, Johannes. *Israel: Its Life and Culture,* 2 vol (London). Vol I tr Mrs. Auslaug Møller, 1926; vol II tr Annie Fausbøll, 1940, reprinted with additions in 1949.

Pritchard, James B. (ed) *Ancient Near Eastern Texts Relating to the Old Testament* (Princeton 1950).

von Rad, Gerhard. *Gesammelte Studien zum Alten Testament,* Theologische Bücherei (Munich 1958). This collection will appear in English as *Collected Old Testament Studies,* tr Dr. Ap-Thomas (New York 1965).

————. *Genesis: A Commentary,* The Old Testament Library, tr John Marks (London 1961).

————. *Old Testament Theology: The Theology of Israel's Historical Traditions,* vol I, tr D. M. G. Stalker (New York 1962).

————. *Studies in Deuteronomy,* tr David Stalker, Studies in Biblical Theology 9 (Chicago 1953).

Robert, Andre and Feuillet, Andre (eds) *Introduction à la Bible,* 2 vol (Tournai, vol I, 2 ed, 1959; vol II, 1st ed, 1958).

Rowley, H. H. *The Biblical Doctrine of Election* (London 1950).

————. *From Joseph to Joshua: Biblical Traditions in the Light of Archaeology,* Schweich Lectures 1948 (London 1950).

————. (ed) *The Old Testament and Modern Study* (Oxford 1951).

de Vaux, Roland. *Ancient Israel: Its Life and Institutions,* tr John McHugh (New York 1961).

————. *La genèse,* La Sainte Bible de Jérusalem (Paris 1951).

Weiser, Artur. *Introduction to the Old Testament,* tr from the 4th German ed by Dorothea Brandon (London 1961).

Wellhausen, Julius. *Prolegomena to the History of Israel,* tr Menzies and Black (New York 1957).

Willoughby, Harold R. (ed) *The Study of the Bible Today and Tomorrow* (Chicago 1947).

Wright, G. Ernest. *Biblical Archaeology* (Philadelphia 1957).

————. *The Old Testament Against Its Environment,* Studies in Biblical Theology (Chicago 1950).

————. (ed) *The Bible and the Ancient Near East: Essays in Honor of William Foxwell Albright* (Garden City 1961).

————. and Freedman, David Noel. *The Biblical Archaeologist Reader* (Garden City 1961).

## Articles

Ahern, Barnabas M. "Exodus, Then and Now," *The Bridge, I: A Yearbook of Judaeo-Christian Studies,* 53–74.

Albright, William F. "Abram the Hebrew: A New Archaeological Interpretation," BASOR 163 (1961) 36–54.

————. "The High Place in Ancient Palestine," VTS 4 (1957) 242–58.

―――. "The Israelite Conquest of Canaan in the Light of Archaeology," BASOR 74 (1939) 11–23.

―――. "Yahweh Sabā'ôt," JBL 67 (1948) 377–81.

Audet, Jean-Paul. "Love and Marriage in the Old Testament," tr F. Burke, Scr 10 (1958) 65–83.

Barr, James. "Revelation Through History in the Old Testament and in Modern Theology," Interpr 17 (1963) 193–98.

Bea, Augustin. "Der heutige Stand der Bibelwissenschaft," SZ 153 (1953–54) 91–104.

―――. "Der heutige Stand der Pentateuchfrage," Bib 16 (1935) 175–200.

Blair, Edward P. "An Appeal to Remembrance," Interpr 15 (1961) 41–47.

Bodenheimer, F. S. "The Manna of Sinai," BA 10 (1947) 2–6. Printed also in The Biblical Archaeologist Reader, ed G. Ernest Wright and David Noel Freedman, 76–80.

Bourke, Myles M. "Yahweh, the Divine Name," The Bridge, III, 271–87.

Bright, John. "Has Archaeology Found Evidence of the Flood?" BA 5 (1942) 55–62. Printed also in The Biblical Archaeologist Reader, 32–40.

―――. "Modern Study of Old Testament Literature," The Bible and the Ancient Near East, ed G. Ernest Wright (Garden City 1957) 13–31.

Cazelles, Henri. "À propos du Pentateuque," Bib 35 (1954) 279–98.

Coppens, Joseph. "L'interpretation sexuelle du péché du Paradis," ETL 24 (1948) 395–439.

―――. "Moïse et les origines du Pentateuque selon M. Cazelles," ETL 32 (1956) 275–81.

―――. "Le Protoévangile," ETL 26 (1950) 5–36.

Cross, Frank M. "The Tabernacle," BA 10 (1947) 45–68. Printed also in The Biblical Archaeologist Reader, 201–28.

Culley, R. C., "An Approach to the Problem of Oral Tradition," VT 13 (1963) 113–25.

Dougherty, John J. "The Origins of Hebrew Religion: A Study in Method," CBQ 17 (1955) 258–76.

Dreyfus, F. "La thème de l'héritage dans l'Ancien Testament," RScPhTh 42 (1958) 582–94.

Dubarle, A. M. "Original Sin in Genesis," DowR 76 (1958) 223–49.

———. "La signification du nom de Iahweh," RScPhTh 35 (1951) 3–21.

Dyson, R. A. "Apropos of a New Study of Genesis," Bib 35 (1954) 225–29.

Eichrodt, Walther. "The Law and the Gospel," tr Charles F. McRae, Interpr 11 (1957) 23–40.

Eissfeldt, Otto. "Modern Criticism," *Record and Revelation,* ed H. Wheeler Robinson (Oxford 1938) 74–90.

Freedman, David Noel. "The Name of the God of Moses," JBL 79 (1960) 151–56.

Gemser, B. "The Importance of the Motive Clause in Old Testament Law," VTS 1 (1953) 50–66.

Gordis, Robert. "The Knowledge of Good and Evil in the Old Testament and the Qumran Scrolls," JBL 76 (1957) 123–38.

Gordon, Cyrus H. "Biblical Customs and the Nuzu Tablets," BA 3 (1940) 1–12.

Guidi, Ignazio. "L'historiographie chez les Sémites," RB 3 (1906) 509–19.

Gunkel, Hermann. "The 'Historical Movement' in the Study of Religion," ExpT 38 (1927) 532–36.

Haelvoet, Marcel. "La théophanie du Sinaï," ETL 29 (1953) 375–97.

Haran, Menahem. "Shiloh and Jerusalem: The Origin of the Priestly Tradition in the Pentateuch," JBL 81 (1962) 14–24.

Hartman, Louis. "The Enumeration of the Ten Commandments," CBQ 7 (1945) 105–08.

Hyatt, J. P. "Yahweh as 'The God of My Father,' " VT 5 (1955) 130–36.

Keszler, Werner. "Der literarische–, historische–, and theologische Problematik des Dekalogs," VT 7 (1957) 1–16.

Lack, Remí. "Les origines de 'Elyôn, le Très-Haut, dans la tradition cultuelle d'Israel," CBQ 24 (1962) 44–64.

Lagrange, M. Joseph. "L'authenticité mosaïque de la Genèse et la théorie des documents," RB 47 (1938) 163–83.

———. "La décret 'Lamentabili' et la critique historique," RB 4 (1907) 543–54.

———. "Les sources du Pentateuque," RB 7 (1898) 10–32.

Lambert, G. "Le drame du jardin d'Eden," NRT 76 (1954) 917–48, 1044–72.

Lambert, W. G. "New Light on the Babylonian Flood," JSemS 5 (1960) 113–23.

Lehmann, Manfred. "Abraham's Purchase of Machphelah and Hittite Law," BASOR 129 (1953) 15–18.

Lohfink, Norbert. "Die Bundesurkunde des Königs Josias," Bib 44 1963) 261–88.

MacKenzie, R. A. F. "Before Abraham Was . . . ," CBQ 15 (1953) 131–40.

———. "The Divine Soliloquies in Gn," CBQ 17 (1955) 277–86.

MacRae, George. "The Meaning and Evolution of the Feast of Tabernacles," CBQ 22 (1960) 251–76.

Maly, Eugene. "Gn 12, 10–20; 20, 1–18; 26, 7–11 and the Pentateuchal Question," CBQ 18 (1956) 255–62.

McCree, Walter T. "The Covenant Meal in the Old Testament," JBL 45 (1926) 120–28.

McKenzie, John L. "God and Nature in the Old Testament," CBQ 14 (1952) 18–39, 125–45.

———. "The Hebrew Attitude Toward Mythological Polytheism," CBQ 14 (1952) 323–35.

———. "Literary Characteristics of Gn 2–3," TS 15 (1954) 541–72.

———. "Myth and the Old Testament," CBQ 21 (1959) 265–82.

———. "The Sacrifice of Isaac," Scr 9 (1957) 79–84.

Meek, Theophile. "Monotheism and the Religion of Israel," JBL 61 (1942) 21–43.

Mendenhall, George E. "Ancient Oriental and Biblical Law," BA 17 (1954) 26–46.

———. "Biblical History in Transition," *The Bible and the Ancient Near East* 32–53.

———. "Covenant Forms in Israelite Tradition," BA 17 (1954) 50–76.

Morgenstern, Julius. "The Oldest Document of the Hexateuch," HUCA 4 (1927) 1–138.

Muilenburg, James. "Form and Structure of the Covenantal Formulations," VT 9 (1959) 347–65.

Meyers, Jacob M. "The Requisite of Response: On the Theology of Dt," Interpr 15 (1961) 14–31.

North, Christopher R. "The Essence of Idolatry," BZAW 77 (1958) 151–60.

————. "Pentateuchal Criticism," *The Old Testament and Modern Study*, 48–83.

North, Robert. "Date and Unicity of the Exodus," AER 134 (1956) 161–82.

O'Callaghan, Roger. "Historical Parallels to Patriarchal Social Customs," CBQ 6 (1944) 391–405.

O'Doherty, Eamonn. "The 'Conjectures' of Jean Astruc," CBQ 15 (1953) 300–04.

Oppenheim, A. Leo. "The Mesopotamian Temple," BA 7 (1944) 54–63. Printed also in *The Biblical Archaeologist Reader,* 158–69.

Pfeiffer, Robert H. "A Non-Israelite Source for the Book of Genesis," ZAW 48 (1930) 66–73.

————. "The Oldest Decalogue," JBL 43 (1924) 294–310.

van der Ploeg, J., "Studies in Hebrew Law," CBQ 12 (1950) 248–59, 416–27; 13 (1951) 28–43, 164–71, 296–307.

von Rad, Gerhard. "Ancient Word and Living Word: The Preaching of Dt and Our Preaching," tr Lloyd Gaston, Interpr 15 (1961) 3–13.

————. Reply to G. Ernest Wright, ExpT 72 (1960–61) 213–16.

Rowley, H. H. "The Antiquity of Israelite Monotheism," ExpT 61 (1949–50) 333–38.

————. "Moses and the Decalogue," BJRylL 34 (1951) 81–118.

————. "Recent Discoveries and the Patriarchal Age," BJRylL 32 (1949–50) 44–79.

————. "The Unity of the Old Testament," BJRylL 29 (1946) 326–58.

Siegman, Edward F. "The Decrees of the Pontifical Biblical Commission: A Recent Clarification," CBQ 18 (1956) 23–29.

Smart, James D. "The Death and Rebirth of Old Testament Theology," JR 23 (1943) 1–11, 125–36.

Speiser, E. A. "The Biblical Idea of History in Its Common Near Eastern Setting," IsrEJ 7 (1957) 201–16.

Vaccari, Alberto. "De questione mosaica," VD 17 (1937) 371–73.

————. "La questione mosaica e la filologia," *L'Osservatore Romano,* Sept. 23, 1937.

Volz, Paul, and Rudolph, Wilhelm. "Der Elohist als Erzähler: Ein Irrweg der Pentateuchkritik?" BZAW 63 (1933) 1–183.

Worden, Thomas. "The Ark of the Covenant," Scr 5 (1952) 82–90.

Wright, G. Ernest. "Archaeology and Old Testament Studies," JBL 77 (1958) 39–55.

———. "History and the Patriarchs," ExpT 71 (1959–60) 292–96.

———. "The Levites in Deuteronomy," VT 4 (1954) 325–30.

———. "Recent European Study of the Pentateuch," JBR 18 (1950) 216–25.

———. "The Terminology of Old Testament Religion and Its Significance," JNES 1 (1942) 404–14.

## Dictionaries

Cazelles, Henri. "Loi israélite," VDBS 5 (1957) 497–530.

———. "Moïse," VDBS 5 (1957) 1307–37.

———. "Mythe et l'Ancien Testament," VDBS 5 (1957) 240–52.

———. "Les patriarches," VDBS 7 (1961) 82–156.

———. and van der Born, A. "Mose," Bibel-Lexikon 1 (1951) 1160–69.

Mowinckel, Sigmund. "Mythos und Mythologie," RGG³ 4 (1960) 1263–78.

Osswald, E. "Moses," RGG³ 4 (1960) 1151–55.

Robert, André. "Littéraires (Genres)," VDBS 4 (1949) 405–21.

Touzard, J. "Moïse et Josué," DAFC 3 (1919) 695–755.

Venard, L. "Historique (Genre)," VDBS 4 (1949) 7–32.

## Papal Documents

Leo XIII. Providentissimus Deus, ASS 26 (1893–94) 269–92.

Pius X. Lamentabili, ASS 40 (1907) 470–78.

———. Pascendi, ASS 40 (1907) 593–650.

———. Praestantia Scripturae Sacrae, ASS 40 (1907) 723–26.

Pius XII. Divino afflante Spiritu, AAS 35 (1943) 297–325.

———. Humani generis, AAS 42 (1950) 561–78.

The Pontifical Biblical Commission. "On Mosaic Authorship of the Pentateuch," ASS 39 (1906) 377–78.

———. "On the Historical Character of the First Three Books of Moses," AAS 1 (1909) 567–69.

———. "Concerning Mosaic Authenticity," AAS 12 (1920) 158.

———. "Reply to Cardinal Suhard," AAS 40 (1948) 45–48.

## Translations of Ancient Near Eastern Lists

Goetze, Albrecht. "Hittite Treaties," ANET 201–03, 203–06.
————. "The Laws of Eshnunna," AASOR 3 (1956).
Meek, Theophile. "The Code of Hammurabi," ANET 163–80.
————. "The Middle Assyrian Laws," ANET 180–88.
Oppenheim, A. Leo. "Sumerian King Lists," ANET 264–66.
Speiser, E. A. "Enuma elish," ANET 60–72.
————. "The Gilgamesh Epic," ANET 72–99.
————. "The Legend of Sargon," ANET 119.
Wilson, John A. "The God and His Unknown Name of Power," ANET 12–14.
————. "Egyptian Creation Myths," ANET 3–4.
————. "Egyptian Treaty," ANET 199–201.
————. "The Story of the Two Brothers," ANET 23–25.

# Biblical References

208

| | | | | | |
|---|---|---|---|---|---|
| 18 | | 129 | | 1–5 | 92 |
| 18 | 1–5 | 130 | | 2–3 | 96 |
| | 6–30 | 110 | | 4 | 93 |
| | 9 | 50 | | 6–21 | 105, 113, |
| | 11 | 50 | | | 122 |
| | 22–30 | 130 | | 23–26 | 92 |
| 19 | | 123, 129 | 6 | | 73, 90, 138 |
| 19 | 2 | 129 | | 6 | 140 |
| | 3–12 | 129 | | 21 | 75 |
| | 13–18 | 129 | | 21–23 | 73 |
| 20 | | 125, 129 | | 21ff | 90 |
| 20 | 10–26 | 110 | 7 | | 138 |
| 21 | | 129 | | 7–8 | 139 |
| 23 | 5 | 144 | | 22 | 96 |
| | 43 | 73 | 8 | 1–2 | 140 |
| | | | | 2 | 140 |

### Deuteronomy

| | | | | | |
|---|---|---|---|---|---|
| | | | | 3 | 87 |
| 1–11 | | 138 | | 4 | 84 |
| 1–27 | | 117 | | 11 | 140 |
| 1 | 6 | 138 | 9 | | 138 |
| | 26–40 | 87 | | 7 | 140 |
| | 31 | 84 | | 13 | 88 |
| | 33 | 85 | 10 | | 138 |
| 4 | 1 | 138 | | 5 | 134 |
| | 9–13 | 140 | | 19 | 73 |
| | 9–15 | 92 | | 22 | 96 |
| | 11 | 92 | 11 | | 138 |
| | 12 | 93 | | 6 | 88 |
| | 13 | 93 | | 26 | 15 |
| | 19 | 29 | 12 | | 138 |
| | 20 | 72 | 12–18 | | 132 |
| | 25–31 | 182 | 12–26 | | 99, 105 |
| | 34 | 23 | | | 131, 132, |
| | 37–38 | 96 | | | 148 |
| | 39–40 | 140 | 12 | 8–10 | 137 |
| | 44 | 111 | | 11 | 133 |
| | 45 | 111 | 14 | 3ff | 136 |
| 5 | | 138 | | 22–27 | 137 |
| | 1 | 15, 138 | | 23 | 133 |

213

## Psalms

| 78 | 12ff | 72 |
| 89 | 10–11 | 97 |
| 104 | 7–9 | 97 |
| 106 | | 90 |
| 135 | 8–9 | 72 |

## Proverbs

| 16 | 9 | 71 |
| 19 | 21 | 71 |

## Isaias

| 6 | 3 | 130 |
| 51 | 9 | 97 |

## Jeremias

| 2 | 2 | 88 |

## Ezechiel

| 2 | 9 | 181 |
| | 9–10 | 130 |
| 28 | 11–19 | 30 |
| 40–48 | | 181 |

## Osee

| 2 | 16–17b | 89 |
| 8 | 11 | 132 |
| 9 | 10 | 88 |
| 11 | 1 | 72 |
| | 1–2 | 88 |

## Micah

| 6 | 4 | 72 |

## Mark

| 14 | 24 | 94 |

## Luke

| 10 | 25ff | 142 |

## Acts

| 3 | 25 | 46 |
| 7 | 22 | 75 |

## Galatians

| 3 | 8 | 46 |

# Index

217